VEGETABLE GARDENS

VEGETABLE

GARDENS

Mimi
Luebbermann

National Home
Gardening Club
Minnetonka, Minnesota

ABOUT THE AUTHOR

Growing vegetables has always been a part of my life. As a small child, I recall walking between rows of tomatoes that stretched up high beyond my vision, their distinctive smell surrounding me like perfume. A stronger memory is the long, wide asparagus bed next to the clothesline, with new heads just poking up in early spring. Standing next to my stooping father, I held the basket to receive the stalks as he worked down the rows cutting the asparagus—the pride of his garden—for dinner. Our tomatoes were canned for the winter, jars of them stretching across the yellow linoleum-topped kitchen table.

Living in California in the seventies, I began to rediscover fresh vegetables when I started to cook for my infants. I tasted again the sweet, true, singing flavor of a vine-ripened tomato, and planted as many fruit trees as I could fit in a small, urban garden, leaving just enough space for a jungle of zucchini vines tangled with pumpkins and sunflowers. After the babies grew up and moved out, I packed up some twenty-plus years of urban living and moved to the country with space for an orchard, a real tomato garden, and indeed, my own asparagus bed.

As with all the most rewarding pursuits, gardening remains a challenge. I am still learning, still working the soil, still experimenting. Gardening is a fine balance of practice and happenstance. The more you garden, the more you improve. I've learned that if plants don't do well, try a different variety or move the plant. Peculiarly, two feet west of its present location it may thrive. And as a gardener I can say, above all: Don't give up! Keep notes, continue to try out new varieties and never be bored. The reward is fresh, wholesome food you have grown yourself. What could taste better?

Mimi Luebbermann

Vegetable Gardens

Printed in 2011.

Tom Carpenter
Creative Director

Julie Cisler
Book Design & Production

Michele Teigen
Senior Book Development Coordinator

Gina Germ
Photo Editor

Michael Landis
Photography

9 10 / 13 12 11
ISBN 10: 1-58159-035-0
ISBN 13: 978-1-58159-035-7
© 1999 National Home Gardening Club

National Home Gardening Club
12301 Whitewater Drive
Minnetonka, Minnesota 55343
www.gardeningclub.com

CONTENTS

◖ CHAPTER 1 ◗
WHY GROW VEGETABLES?

Picture a fine vegetable garden: the first blush of ripening tomatoes on tall vines; teepees of vines festooned with yellow, green or purple snap beans; meandering pumpkin vines punctuated with orange globes; purple, pink or even white eggplants hanging off bushes and looking almost like Christmas tree ornaments.

Or imagine: bright red- and green-leafed lettuces alternating down a row, as beautiful as an Oriental rug; buzzing bumblebees nuzzling inside zucchini blossoms, emerging dusted with yellow pollen; strolling past and brushing against a row of basil plants, setting off a fragrance that escorts you down the row.

The vegetable garden certainly provides many pleasures for your eyes, nose and ears. But the biggest reward may be the pleasure you will get from eating the bounty of your land.

Whether you grow them in raised beds or in a special patch, nothing beats the taste of homegrown vegetables.

Mix flowers with vegetables to make them both look better. Even humble cauliflower and lettuce have ornamental qualities.

A couple decades ago, just about everyone with even the smallest patch of ground grew a few vegetables. Neighbors compared the growth spurts of their tomatoes, shared vegetables and talked about bugs and watering techniques as they leaned over the back fence or stopped to chat on the front sidewalk. Sharing seeds, saved from year to year, was as much a part of the harvest as picking the lettuce for dinner.

Today's backyard gardens come in smaller and smaller sizes, if there at all, and most people work long hours outside the home. It seems easier to buy vegetables at the local store. Yet store-bought vegetables pale, in almost every way, when compared to homegrown.

The joy of harvesting your own homegrown food is unquestionable. Mass-produced vegetables shipped from far away often suffer from tastelessness and soggy texture. Strolling down the aisles of your homegrown tomato rows provides more satisfaction than trudging down the aisle of sad imitations in the local supermarket.

Since we descended from farmers and vegetable gardeners who tilled the soil for eons before us, many of us feel the need to reconnect with the seasons and the soil, whether harvesting from a couple large terra-cotta containers or a three acre garden.

Besides the vegetable garden's aesthetics, there are a number of practical reasons to grow vegetables in your own backyard.

The importance of wholesome, nourishing food cannot be challenged, so knowing exactly where your food grows gives you the assurance it has been raised with safe gardening practices. Picked fresh from the garden and walked to the kitchen, your homegrown

Growing vegetables in long rows gives you a chance to harvest methodically, and interplant with flowers and herbs.

Yes, you can enjoy the beauty, bounty and flavor of homegrown veggies for months with a few simple canning techniques.

For variety—golden, pink, purple, striped; elongated or round; carrot-sized or radish-sized—these can't be "beet."

Don't forget edible flowers as part of your vegetable garden. Pansies make colorful garnishes to side dishes and salads.

vegetables are guaranteed to be packed full of vitamins and minerals, unlike the pale replicas picked green and ripened artificially. With the drop in home vegetable gardens, the per capita consumption of fruits and vegetables has declined by almost half in the last fifty years, while the incidence of cancer has risen. The National Council on Health urges Americans to eat more fresh vegetables, and when an appealing variety is just a step from the kitchen it is easy to add more to your dinner menu.

Gardening brings together all family and household members

in a mutual endeavor. Waist-high beds can be constructed for those physically handicapped or for gardeners who find stooping and bending difficult or painful. Even if kids resist weeding (a resistance many grown-ups share), they love to harvest; picking becomes fun, not a task.

A garden is the perfect classroom for children to learn how plants grow. They can plant a tiny bean, corn or radish seed and watch the plant grow, mature and produce. And by observing butterflies as they land on the flowers of a pineapple mint to suck out the sweet nectar, children learn how other creatures feed themselves. These children in particular will suddenly start eating their vegetables, and carrots, green beans and sugar snap peas might even be consumed right off the vine.

It's a simple fact: If children watch plants grow, they take a greater interest in the harvest, from the garden all the way to the plate.

You don't need a large space to grow vegetables. Even a tiny garden will produce surprising quantities of food. Containers overflowing with lettuce and scallions provide fresh salads night after night. Just one or two summer squash plants will have you knocking at your neighbor's door to share the harvest. Three or four different herbs can flavor your food with a variety of fresh savory notes. Lettuce grows tidily next to zinnias, and corn planted behind a perennial border can add its own beauty, especially the heirloom types with bronze-purple leaves.

Preserving gives the gardener a year-round supply of home-grown vegetables. Dried veg-

etable chips make great snacks, and your own popcorn tastes far superior to any store-bought types. Whether you have a large freezer or a couple of shelves filled with canned tomatoes and pickles, their bright and fresh tastes will remind you of summer's generous bounty in the midst of winter.

There are so many reasons to grow vegetables. In every way, it is a pastime that will appeal to all your senses and provide satisfaction to your gardening soul in every season.

Vegetables and their growing habits can fascinate both kids and adults. Here, a globe artichoke displays its exotic (and delicious) heads.

Swiss chard, a relative of the beet, is another nutritious vegetable that doubles as an ornamental.

◀ CHAPTER 2 ▶

GROWING VEGETABLES: A PRACTICAL GUIDE

There's much more to growing vegetables than just popping a few seeds into the ground, or running to the nursery for a few seedlings to throw into the dirt, and hoping for the best. Not that vegetable gardening is or should be complex; it isn't. But there a few key planning, preparation and plant care strategies you need to know and use. That's what this chapter is all about.

In addition, you'll find several complete Garden Plans here—full-fledged ideas for specialty gardens you may want to create in the gardening space you have.

Through it all, remember that vegetable gardening should be fun. To be sure, there is reward in the outcome—delicious food on the table. But remember that time in the garden is time well-spent for reflection and rejuvenating the spirit—another set of great rewards.

BEFORE DIGGING IN: PLANNING YOUR GARDEN

Once the spring sunshine clears away winter's clouds and the warmth of the sun makes daffodils peek up through the soil, gardeners get the itch to start planting. Drawing up even a minimal plan helps assure success. So before digging in, consider the size of garden you can maintain, the right plants for each season's weather, and the best location for your plants. A bit of planning can save a bucket load of work, and generate results.

Gardening should never be a chore, but a pleasure and an avocation. Without a plan, it is quite easy to plant and plant and plant, ultimately to the gardener's undoing. A garden too large can be overwhelming, both for maintenance and for harvest. Before taking up the shovel, take a little time to consider the amount of time you have to garden, and scale your efforts accordingly.

Planning Ideas

- **Poll your household** for suggestions of favorite vegetables. If everyone has a stake in the process, everyone will lend a hand.

Knowing what kind of shade you have will help you match your plants to your site. Many vegetables and herbs will take some shade. Lettuce, for example, will need shade in hotter weather.

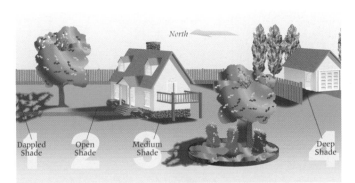

- **Assess your garden site** for the amount of sun it receives every day and in different seasons. For example, lettuce, cherry tomatoes and some herbs can cope with a bit of filtered summer shade. Melons and corn tolerate only 1 to 2 hours of shade. Plant each type of vegetable according to the amount of sun it requires.

- **Test your soil** for pH and nutrients, then build and adjust it to fill your plants' needs.

- **If space is limited,** consider concrete areas, decks or driveways for container vegetable gardens. Sunny flower or shrub borders can be interplanted with herbs, lettuces and edible flowers.

The best garden plans grow out of several seasons of experimenting. By trying different varieties, moving beds from one spot to another and through trial and error,

you can learn which plants suit the growing seasons in your garden's microclimate. Sketch a tentative plan and look over your seeds from last summer. Many seeds are viable for more than one year, although the percentage of germination diminishes from year to year. (Seed sources listed on page 154.)

Whether you are planning your first garden or your fiftieth, keep a garden journal to help you plan a better garden every year. Note the varieties you planted, the date you planted them and the first day of harvest. By doing this you can judge how your garden performs in your particular spot, and get insights into adjustments and improvements you might make.

Keep a garden journal to track your success. Make a note of how well vegetable varieties do, so you'll know what to grow next year.

ANNUAL, PERENNIAL, BIENNIAL

Plants have different growing cycles. Annuals grow, bloom and form seed in one growing season. Biennials sprout, grow and bloom in two growing seasons before setting seed. Perennials are the long-lived members, coming up year after year in the garden.

Planning for the Growing Seasons

When planning your garden, match plants with the temperature levels of your seasons. For example, many lettuces with delicate leaves thrive in cool and moist spring temperatures, but with a whiff of summer's heat, they bolt (send up a flower stalk).

As the weather cools in the fall, lettuces flourish again until the nip of frost ends the season. Zucchini seeds planted in cold soil sulk, refusing to grow until hot days and warm nights encourage growth. Rutabagas and parsnips wait for a touch of fall frost to complete the sugar production that sweetens their roots.

Within each season there are plants of the same type that grow more quickly, while others take longer. Vegetables are labeled early, mid- and late-season to denote how long it takes them to produce. An 'Early Girl' tomato, tolerant of cool evening temperatures, blossoms and begins to produce quicker than a

Lettuce doesn't have to grow in long rows. Try using it as an ornamental and edible border plant in the veggie patch, or even the flower patch.

beefsteak type that requires hot days and nights to stimulate bloom.

As an example of an early season tomato, 'Early Girl' has a harvest date of 54 days, while the late season 'Hybrid Beefmaster' takes 80 days to produce its first plump, red tomato. But take note: Seed producers set the harvest days according to their own growing trials. Your harvest dates will vary from their's due to the variations in your garden's microclimate.

Early-season varieties are suited for gardens with cool summers or those in the North with short season gardens. Mid- and late-season varieties can thrive in more temperate areas with longer growing seasons. If your growing season is 90 days or longer, you can plant early-, mid- and late-season types for a long succession of harvest.

Growing Types: Bush vs. Vining

For small gardens, "bush" type plants take less space and are also good candidates for containers. On these plants, flowers appear almost simultaneously; once they have set seed, they do not continue to produce.

Sowing a succession of bush plants every two to three weeks prolongs the harvest for bush-type varieties. However, as long as the fruits of the larger "vining" types are picked regularly, they will continue to flower and produce over a long season.

COMPANION PLANTING

There is a great deal of mystique and folklore about companion planting. Articles tout placing plants friendly to each other side-by-side, which supposedly stimulates both plants to grow better. For instance, carrots are supposed to be friendly with potatoes. This concept has not been scientifically proven.

Sometimes companion planting means growing certain flowering plants near a vegetable garden to encourage beneficial insects which prey on garden pests. One example: The syrphid fly in particular likes buckwheat,

which is also valuable as a grain. This fly then preys upon aphids, leafhoppers and mealybugs.

On the other hand, plants with strong smelling leaves or blossoms—like marigolds, nasturtiums, catnip, yarrow and zinnias—can discourage certain insects.

You can interplant herbs and flowers in any vegetable bed. Their strong fragrances often help deter insects too.

Raised beds are terrific for both vegetables and flowers, because you can control the soil content and give different plants the drainage they like.

MAXIMIZING RESULTS: SOIL, FERTILIZER AND MORE

All gardens benefit from plenty of organic matter. You can dig in ready-bagged compost or make your own. In either case, your vegetables will grow better.

The Best Environment

For vegetable gardening success, provide an environment that encourages plants to grow quickly from seed to maturity. If you keep a plant growing at its optimal rate it will grow larger and produce a bigger harvest. To do this, provide plants with all they need: good location, rich soil, proper feeding, smart watering, and adequate weed and pest control.

A plant depends upon the soil for its water and nourishment. Soil is a reservoir of food and drink for your plants. The first step to successful gardening is checking out your garden soil to make sure it delivers the necessary ingredients to assure the health and growth of your plants.

Soils and Potting Mixes

Soil is a mixture of three particles—sand, silt and clay—plus organic matter. The silt, clay and organic matter interact with water in the soil to provide nutrients that the plant's roots absorb. Sand, although chemically inert, plays an important role by creating large spaces between the particles. This allows water to drain, encourages high oxygen concentrations between particles and promotes good vertical water movement.

Organic matter is mostly old plant material in various states of decomposition. Over time, this liberates mineral elements essential for plant growth. Digging compost into the soil improves its composition and encourages good bacteria and fungi, which benefit plants by

Power tilling helps you add soil amendments, and loosens up the soil for planting. If you just use a tiller occasionally, rent one or chip in with neighbors to buy one.

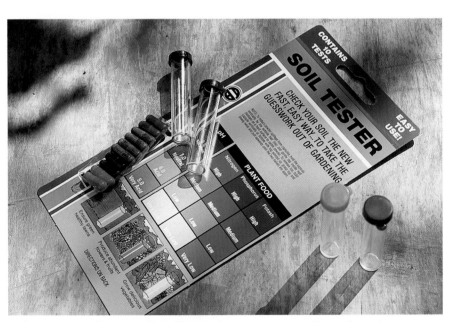

To know your soil's pH and nutrient makeup, request a soil test through your county extension service, or purchase a test kit.

Compost is the best plant food and soil amendment there is, and it's easy to make your own in your own backyard.

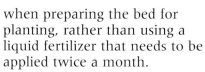

Time-release fertilizer pellets cut down on the frequency of feedings, and they offer a uniform nutrient supply to your plants.

fighting off the bad, disease-causing microorganisms.

A good garden soil crumbles easily in your hand. Healthy soil has a rich earthy smell because of its organic material. Your soil should have this good smell, and you should see small bits of decomposed compost among the soil's grains when you look closely. Your spade should slide into the ground easily, and water in a planting hole should drain out slowly but steadily. A good soil produces strong, healthy plants that grow quickly.

For container plantings, use a good-quality potting mix. Don't use garden soil in containers; by late summer it will form itself into a solid, concrete-hard mass. Commercial potting mixes have been sterilized, which makes them cleaner than decomposing materials for growing plants indoors.

Fertilizers and pH Balance

Finding the right nutritional balance encourages peak performance from any plants. Too much nitrogen and they grow too fast, becoming long, lank and more susceptible to disease and insect problems. Tomatoes, if given too much nitrogen, put on a burst of leaf growth but don't flower: You get huge tomato trees without tomatoes. With no nitrogen, beans sit stunted in the soil, barely growing.

The major nutrients needed for plant growth are nitrogen, phosphorus and potassium (symbolized by the letters N, P and K). A plant removes these nutrients from the soil and uses them to grow. Adding fertilizer to the soil replaces the missing or used-up nutrients, allowing the plant to continue its growth. Because nutrient needs are greatest during periods of rapid growth, fertilize your beds when you are preparing them for planting.

Commercial fertilizers list their contents as the percentage of each nutrient, in the order of nitrogen-phosphorus-potassium. For example, an NPK formula of 10-10-10 has equal percentages of nitrogen, phosphorus and potassium. Some gardeners prefer timed-release, organic, pelleted fertilizers for their vegetable gardens. Add the pellets

when preparing the bed for planting, rather than using a liquid fertilizer that needs to be applied twice a month.

Some plants need the extra boost of liquid fertilizer monthly during their growing season in addition to the fertilizer introduced to the planting bed.

Plant growth also depends upon soil chemistry. The pH (potential hydrogen) balance of the soil affects how well a plant absorbs nutrients from the soil. Acid soils have a pH of 6.9 and lower; alkaline soils have a pH of 7.1 and higher. Every gardener should purchase an inexpensive soil pH tester, available at garden centers and hardware stores. One of the simplest designs has probes and indicates on the dial the soil's pH. Using the soil tester, you can make sure the pH is adjusted to the needs of the plants ... or focus on plants that will thrive in the pH for the soil you have been given.

TIP ORGANIC ALTERNATIVES

Consider using organic fertilizers in your garden. Choose the new brands with NPK formulas in time-release pellets. Many gardeners testify to the improved taste of the produce. Liquid fish fertilizer, another organic alternative, has now been deodorized and gives plants a hearty boost of nitrogen.

Granular fertilizers are usually partially soluble. If you add them to a new bed a few weeks before planting, they will release their nutrients in time to help new plants.

WATERING PRACTICES

Water is essential for the growth of plants—both as a carrier of nutrients from the soil, and as a circulation medium much like blood in the human body. When plants absorb water through their roots, the water carries nutrients from the soil to the leaves. As water evaporates through pores in the leaves, the roots draw more water from the soil, like straws sucking up liquid.

On hot or windy days—periods of high evaporation—the rate of water loss from the leaves increases, so the roots need more water. When the leaves lose more water than the roots can quickly replenish, the plant wilts. A properly watered plant is one that has constant access to readily available water in the soil. So when temperatures soar, increase your watering.

Irrigation channels are a time-tested way to get water to larger numbers of plants. Be careful not to erode the soil with a heavy volume of water.

Drainage is Important

Soil composition affects the amount of water available for plants and the health of their roots.

Very sandy soil drains quickly, so plants have less water available. Clay soils drain less readily but may be too heavy and compacted for healthy root growth. The air in the spaces between soil particles contains the same gases as does our atmosphere, including oxygen vital for healthy plants. When the spaces between particles of soil are filled with water, oxygen is pushed out and consequently is not available to the roots. Just as plants can die from too little water, they can die from too much.

When a good-quality garden loam fills with water, gravity pulls the water down through the spaces between the

soil particles, allowing oxygen to fill them again. Factors such as heavy clay soil, the lack of a hole in a planting container, or a layer of rocks at the bottom of a pot, prevent proper drainage; plant roots suffocate.

Incorporating plenty of organic matter—in the form of compost, well-rotted leafmold, peat moss, and the like—to your garden beds before planting is an excellent way to encourage water penetration and retention no matter what kind of soil you have. In sandy soils, the organic matter retains moisture; compost absorbs water like a sponge, holding it available for plant roots. In clay soils, the organic matter breaks up the clay particles, creating spaces through which water can drain and oxygen can refill.

Direct watering at ground level keeps foliage dry and less prone to disease. When using a hose with no nozzle, take care not to erode the soil.

A dispersing sprinkler spreads a fine mist over a broad area, but a higher percentage of the water will evaporate than if you water at ground level.

Different Watering Techniques

Virtually every garden needs some type of system to deliver enough water for plants to quickly grow into their production cycles. Good systems match the needs of the plants with a means of easy delivery. Erratic watering, with periods of wet alternating with drought, has a negative effect on vegetable growth patterns, production and flavor.

Drip Irrigation

A drip irrigation system is one of the best methods to water plants for most gardens, because it delivers a consistent amount of water to the plants at a rate they can readily absorb. In locations with minimal summer rains, a drip system uses less water more effectively than a traditional overhead irrigation system. Such a system can be as simple as soaker hoses run off a faucet, or as elaborate as a

Young vegetable plants in pots need hand watering. Test for dryness by putting your index finger in the soil. If the top $1/2$ inch of the soil is dry, it's a good time to water.

system of small lines run off automatically-timed electronic valves.

If you are installing a system yourself, the variety of parts may at first seem overwhelming. But with the help of a good book specializing in irrigation, you'll discover that the process is quite simple—almost like playing with tinker toys. A simple system can also be set up for containers.

Traditional Watering

In areas with plenty of water, traditional overhead watering works well. However, with plants prone to mildew such as peas and squash, be sure to water early in the morning to allow the leaves to dry before nightfall.

Overhead rotating sprinklers deliver lots of water to larger areas. With overhead sprinklers, water early in the day so foliage dries by nightfall. This helps prevent mildew and other diseases.

A drip irrigation system brings water right to the plant. Once in place, it will save you water, time and worry. Timer systems let you water plants automatically, even when you're away. Inset: A variety of drip components are available, including metal pipe with holes in it, plastic connectors and emitters, and soaker hoses.

TIP — GAUGING WATERING TIME

Place a small can in your garden when you start overhead watering. After 5 minutes, note the depth of water in the can and dig down in the soil to discover the amount of soil absorption. You will quickly learn to judge how long to water to achieve the soaking most beneficial to your plants.

SETTING UP THE GARDEN

Mounded or raised beds can be showpieces even when planted with the humble onion.

AUTUMN JUMP-START

Savvy gardeners in cold winter areas can get a jump on spring planting. Here's how. Prepare special spring-growing beds in the fall. After the last of the crops are out but before the soil is too wet to work, dig in large quantities of compost and manure, turning the bed and working it to perfect soil composition. Mulch this bed carefully with partially composted organic material to a depth of 6 inches. In the spring, remove the mulch and plant early-spring root crops and lettuces directly into the beds.

A good, friable (crumbly) soil is easy to work with. Here, hills are being formed for pumpkins and squash. The shallow ring will retain water for thirsty vine plants.

Like a house with its furniture, gardens have their own structures to make them comfortable for their inhabitants. The way you set up garden beds, planting mounds and paths makes a garden easy for you to maintain as well as beneficial to the plants.

Preparing the Garden Bed

For garden beds, cultivate the soil two to three weeks before your seeds or transplants are ready to set out. If the soil is so wet that it falls off the shovel in wet clumps, wait until the soil dries some to get started, otherwise it will dry into nearly unbreakable clumps. Turning the soil when it is too wet compacts the soil and may ruin its texture for many seasons to come. Compacted soil has less oxygen so plant roots suffer from oxygen deprivation; your plants will not grow successfully.

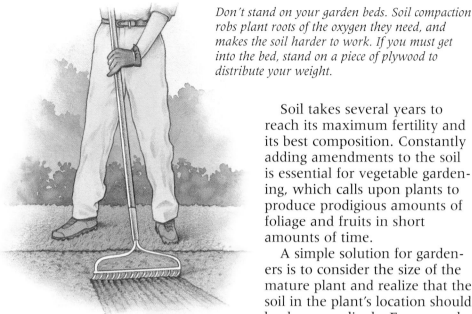

Don't stand on your garden beds. Soil compaction robs plant roots of the oxygen they need, and makes the soil harder to work. If you must get into the bed, stand on a piece of plywood to distribute your weight.

This mounded bed of different varieties of lettuce looks beautiful and drains well too.

Turning the Soil

Although there are gardeners vastly partisan to different methods of digging—techniques called double-digging, single digging or no-till—the main purpose of the activity is simply to loosen the soil and add nutrients for both soil composition and plant nutrition.

Soil takes several years to reach its maximum fertility and its best composition. Constantly adding amendments to the soil is essential for vegetable gardening, which calls upon plants to produce prodigious amounts of foliage and fruits in short amounts of time.

A simple solution for gardeners is to consider the size of the mature plant and realize that the soil in the plant's location should be dug accordingly. For example, globe beets and radishes with short roots need excellent soil composition 8 to 12 inches deep, while deep-rooted tomatoes want 12 to 18 inches of friable (crumbly) soil. Working the bed to the needs of the plant can save a great deal of energy for the gardener.

How to Dig a Bed

To dig beds, start as early as the soil can be worked. Remove existing weeds or plants that you no longer want to grow there. Add at least 4 inches of organic compost, and with a shovel, spade or a machine such as a rototiller, turn over the soil to a depth of 12 to 18 inches. Water the turned soil regularly for the next two weeks to allow any weeds to sprout. Then remove the weeds, using a hoe or shovel to break up any large dirt clods. Rake the surface smooth for planting.

Make the width of your mounds about twice the length of your reach, so you can get to the center from each side. If you plant closer together, plants will form a shady canopy that keeps soil cooler and weeds down.

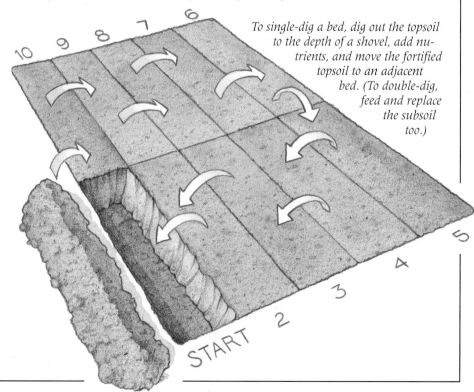

To single-dig a bed, dig out the topsoil to the depth of a shovel, add nutrients, and move the fortified topsoil to an adjacent bed. (To double-dig, feed and replace the subsoil too.)

SEEDS

Starting plants from seed saves you money, and gives you a greater variety of plants to choose from. Plus, you can grow them your way from the get-go. It can become a passion!

Starting your own plants from seed is easy, and offers the advantage of growing a wide range of varieties that nurseries do not regularly stock. If you live in a cold climate with a short growing season, starting seeds inside produces vigorous plants ready for transplanting just as soon as the ground warms up. Seeds also can be sown directly into the ground later, after the warmth of spring has brought the ground temperature up to a level that encourages germination.

Seed Saving

You can order seeds in January, or save your own seeds from year to year—an enjoyable pursuit with practical results: Seeds saved from your garden are adapted to your own microclimate.

In the garden's cycle, plants grow to maturity, blossom and then bear seeds in fruit like berries or tomatoes, in dry pods like peas or beans, or in flower heads and seed pods like love-in-the-mist. Select the best plants— those which grow the largest and appear to have the most plant vigor and health—and pick out the choicest fruits, pods or seed heads to save. Woe be to those who gobble up the largest seed or harvest the most gorgeous flowers

and use the puniest to continue their seed harvest! Pick fruit or seeds from three or more plants to save for the widest genetic base. Remember: Seeds from hybrid plants do not "grow true" to their parents' form (see page 41).

Understanding Pollination

Pollination is the first step in seed production. Most plants carry both male and female reproductive organs—sometimes both occurring in the same blossom (as in a lily) or sometimes, as with squash, in separate male and female flowers.

Self-fertilizing plants (such as beans and lettuce) don't require external fertilization and in some cases can be depended upon to produce pure seed without assistance.

Fertilization becomes a critical issue for gardeners who wish to save pure strains of their heirloom or non-hybrid varieties. If you grow several different varieties of corn, the plots of each variety must be isolated from the other in order to avoid cross-pollination.

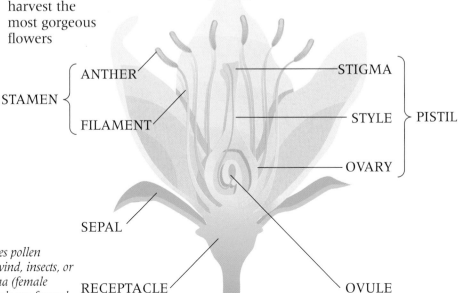

Pollination: The stamen (male part) produces pollen when the anthers ripen and split open. The wind, insects, or even the gardener affix the pollen to the stigma (female part). The pollen reaches the ovary, where seeds are formed.

Managing Your Seed Stock

Here's how to maintain the purity of your seed.

Separate your plants from each other, setting the plots at a distance. Even this doesn't always work, so one way around it is to plant varieties with different maturity dates. For example, planting different varieties of sunflowers successively a month apart allows them to flower and set seed separately.

Should weather factors interfere with your plan so that both the early and the late season variety start to bloom simultaneously, you may need to resort to bagging one type in order to achieve purity of the other.

Bagging means covering the flowers with cloth or paper bags and closing the bottoms tightly so the flowers aren't pollinated by the wind or insects. Order specially treated bags that hold up to the weather from garden suppliers (reference this book's resource section).

Controlling Pollination

Hand-pollinating followed by bagging works on squash and pumpkins. Using a clean, dry paint brush, brush off pollen from the anther of a male flower—the male is just a flower with no indication of fruit—of the same variety or from the anthers on the same plant and brush it on the lips of the stigma. In the case of tomato flowers,

TIP **ADD SOME LIGHT**

If your young plants lean toward their light source and look spindly and weak, they are not getting enough light. Hang grow lights or full-spectrum lights 4 to 6 inches above the containers for compact growth.

Make simple grow-lights from fluorescent fixtures. Use full-spectrum lights, and raise or lower them with ceiling hooks and chains as your plants grow.

you need a small brush, though giant sunflower heads call for a larger brush. After you have pollinated, bag the head of the pollinated flower. Tie the base of the bag securely to prevent insects from crawling up inside.

Some dedicated heirloom gardeners fashion large, light cages with a fine-mesh wire top and sides: Water or rain can trickle in, but insects and foreign pollen are kept out. Row covers from special cloth achieve this same effect as long as the covers are securely fastened at the ends and sides. Use this method only during periods of cool weather, because you should not open the edges of the cover to let heat escape.

Wet and Dry Processing

Seeds develop either in a wet fruit (like a tomato or a squash) or in a dry fruit such as beans. There are different techniques to separate seeds for each group.

Wet Processing

Open the fruit and scrape out the seeds and pulp. Let mixture sit for several

If you grow crops under insect-free fabric, or want to ensure the purity of an heirloom strain, you'll have to hand-pollinate with a small paintbrush.

days to allow fermentation to occur. Keep the seeds dry or they may germinate or be attacked by fungus. When the seeds show no surrounding gel (about 3 to 5 days), add water to the mixture. Seeds that float are not viable, so skim them off.

In a fine sieve, drain off the remaining seeds. Run water vigorously over the seed mixture to wash away any pulp. Dry the seeds as thoroughly as possible, using a paper or cloth towel to wipe the bottom of the sieve. Turn the seeds out into a glass, ceramic or metal dish; do not use paper, which sticks as the seeds dry. Dry the seeds in a warm place, but not in an oven, direct sun or any location where the temperature rises above 96°F.

Dry Processing

Leave podded seeds (like peas and beans) in husks to dry, right on the plant. But in case of impending frost or unseasonable

You don't need a lot of fancy equipment to start your own seeds. Clean recycled materials will work fine.

rain, you may need to uproot the whole plant and hang it in a protected, frost-free, dry space to allow the seeds to ripen and dry fully. In dry climates, leave corn on the stalk to dry. In wetter climates, pick the corn, pull back the husk and discard the silk. String the corn, still on the cob, and hang in a warm, dry space. When dry, leave the corn on the cob or strip off the kernels and store in glass jars.

Seed Storage

With care, many seeds stay viable for years. Keep seeds dry and in a cool dark place. Store in paper or plastic envelopes, but then seal seeds in tightly closed glass jars to protect them from moisture, bugs or rodents. Moisture encourages fungal diseases or may cause the seeds to prematurely sprout.

Record Keeping

Note briefly the source of the plant (e.g. your garden, catalog, neighbor, nursery etc.), the date you received the plant, how successfully the seeds germinated, the plant's productivity and the last growing season. If you give seeds to other gardeners, be sure

Film canisters are great for storing seeds, because they're both water-proof and opaque. But be sure your seeds are thoroughly dry before you store them.

to keep track of their where-abouts. If you lose your harvest, you can beg back seeds for the next year.

Starting Your Seeds

Use seed starting kits such as styrofoam flats, plastic six-packs or peat pots. Choose pots or containers with individual sections for each seedling so that the transplants will pop out of them easily.

Most seeds need temperatures from 65 to 75°F to germinate. Electric heating mats below germinating trays keep the potting mix evenly warm and stimulate growth. A sunny south window may provide enough warmth and light—although young plants take more light than you think.

Start your seeds 6 to 8 weeks before you want to put plants in the garden or into containers. Buy sterilized potting mix or make your own with equal quantities of vermiculite, perlite and peat moss.

Add an all-purpose fertilizer to the mix according to the manufacturer's directions; alternately, when the seedlings develop several pairs of leaves, water them once a week with a liquid fertilizer diluted to half strength.

Before planting seeds, thoroughly moisten the planting mix with water. Sow the seeds at the correct depth. Pat down the mix firmly and water carefully. Keep the mix moist but not soggy—about as damp as a squeezed-out sponge—to discourage fungal infections.

Place seed containers where they get at least four hours or more of bright sun a day, or under hanging grow lights. When roots begin to show at the bottom of the container, the plants are ready to be set outdoors or transplanted into larger containers if conditions are not yet ready in the garden. Do not let your plants become pot-bound, which retards growth.

When starting seeds, use a plastic cover to retain heat and moisture—but remove it when seeds germinate or they'll cook to death.

Always label your seedling containers. It's much easier than guessing what's what after the plants emerge.

PLANTING THE GARDEN

Seedlings are ready to transplant when they show a few sets of true leaves. But first, harden them off for a week or so (see below).

Start lettuce indoors six weeks ahead of when you can work the soil. The heirloom butterhead variety 'Tom Thumb', shown here, is charming, compact and suitable for containers or edgings.

Transplanting Young Plants

Young plants raised indoors or in a greenhouse are tender, so accustom them to the outdoors before you set them in the garden. This process is called hardening off, and here's how to do it:

The week before you plant, set the seedlings outdoors during the day only. Start in the shade, gradually moving them into the sun. When you plant them, do it in the late afternoon to reduce heat stress.

Before planting, submerge the transplants in their containers in a sink or bucket of water until air bubbles cease. To transplant, gently tap the little plant from its container, taking care to keep the root ball and all its potting mix intact. When planting in the garden, leave enough room so plants do not become crowded as they mature.

Make a hole in the planting bed and set the plant in so the top of the root ball is level with the soil. Tamp the soil gently around the root ball, making sure the plant is set securely into the ground. Water consistently until the plants become established and show new growth.

After the seedlings are about 6 inches high, mulch with 1 inch of compost or other organic material. As plants grow larger, increase the mulch to a depth of 3 to 4 inches.

TIP   BOGUS B12

Recent research has shown that vitamin B-12, which was supposed to lessen transplant shock, has no real effect. Watering the plants daily until their feeder roots regrow is the best cure for wilt from transplanting.

How to Transplant

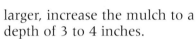

1 Tap the bottom of the container until the root ball comes free. Never tug on a stem.

2 Figure out the right spacing (see the "How to Grow" section for each vegetable in Chapter 3). Set each young plant in a premade hole.

3 Gently tamp down the soil just until any air pockets are gone. Don't tamp too much or soil will compact and hinder the roots' growth.

4 Give your new transplants a good watering. Repeat as needed until they start to take off on their own. (If your soil is heavy and doesn't drain well, don't overwater.)

Direct-sowing of warm weather plants, like the corn shown here, must wait until the soil warms up. (Corn needs a soil temperature of at least 55°F; 65°F for some hybrids.)

Seeding Directly into the Ground

Seed spring gardens early with cool season crops, even when the ground is still cold. But bear in mind that you may have to resow if excessive rains wash out the seeds or rot them. Summer plants such as tomatoes, peppers, eggplant and squash, will not grow successfully until the ground warms up. Do not plant them directly in the soil before night temperatures consistently rise above 50°F.

Row Planting

Thoroughly water the prepared bed 24 hours before planting. For row planting, drag your finger through the prepared moist soil to create a trough the depth specified for the seeds. Sow the seeds in the trough, spacing them as evenly as you can. Cover the trough with soil and pat down firmly. Make additional troughs at distances apart specified for the plants. Water gently so the seeds will not be dislodged.

Keep the bed moist so that a crust will not form on the top, which prevents the seedlings from breaking though.

Bed Planting

To plant a bed, mound up the soil in a square bed that is 2 feet by 2 feet—or the size you prefer—and about 6 inches higher than the normal soil level. The bed should not be more than 4 feet wide, allowing you to reach in from each side. Never walk on a worked bed, or you risk compacting the ground. If you are planting in a raised bed, loosen and rake the soil.

Sow seeds evenly over the bed. Cover the seeds with enough soil so they are at the depth specified for the plants.

Pat the soil down firmly and water gently so the seeds will not be dislodged. Keep the bed moist so that a crust will not form on the top.

Coldframes and Hot Beds

In cold winter areas, gardeners create coldframes to trap early spring warmth and encourage plant growth in young seedlings. Coldframes can run the gamut, from glass windows balanced on cinderblocks to special boxes with hinged lids.

Coldframes and hotbeds give you a jump on the growing season.

Some gardeners make good use of an old-fashioned concept known as hot beds in combination with their coldframes. Here's how to make a hot bed.

In the fall, work the soil under the coldframe. Add four to six inches of fresh manure over the soil. Water thoroughly. Then cover the mixture with another four inches of soil. and water again. In the early spring, as temperatures begin to rise, water again. As the temperature rises, the decomposing manure-rich layer will create bottom heat, warming the soil for the new plants.

Plants spaced too far apart and left unmulched will have to fight weeds that grow in the gaps [left]. With proper spacing and a layer of mulch, you can prevent weeds from taking hold [right].

Spacing

Spacing plants in beds so that the leaves of the plants just touch when mature has special advantages. With this type of spacing, the plants create a mini-environment under their leaves. Water evaporates slower from the soil, so watering is minimized. And the lack of direct sunlight discourages weeds.

But the bed must be rich enough to support such an intensive planting.

Experiment with bed and row planting to help decide which you prefer. If you sow plants such as lettuce or beets thickly in a bed, you can enjoy the immature thinnings in salads.

Successive plantings will ensure that you'll have a steady harvest. Here, a new bed of corn has been planted every two weeks for fresh ears all summer long.

Successive Planting

With quick-producing plants such as radishes, lettuce and edible pod peas, plant a new row every two weeks so you have new plants coming into harvest as the others are diminishing. For vegetables like tomatoes or peppers, planting early-, mid- and late-season varieties all at the same time achieves the effect of successive harvesting.

SPECIAL CARE

Weather affects the amount of water a plant needs. On hot, dry days plants experience higher moisture loss from their leaves (transpiration) and they will need more water to replace what was used. Seedlings are particularly susceptible to hot weather because their roots are not developed enough to absorb the loss of water from their leaves. Water before or after the heat of the day.

CROP ROTATION

Crop rotation can help meet plants' nutritional needs, and can help prevent disease in the garden.

When you work soil amendments in before planting, only some of those nutrients will be taken out. Root crops need large amounts of potassium and phosphorus for their root development, while cucumbers need a lot of nitrogen to grow their long, leafy vines and fruit. By rotating root crops and leaf crops, plants can absorb different nutrients from the soil.

Some plants are more prone to soil-borne disease than others. When they are left in the same position year after year, disease is encouraged to bloom there. Rotation helps prevent this.

Rotation can be simple or complex. You can simply make it a rule to plant tomatoes in one spot one year and then in another spot the next year, but don't plant them in a spot their relatives—potatoes, peppers and eggplants—were the year before.

Intercropping

Most gardeners have more plants they wish to grow than space in the garden. Making use of space left empty while plants are maturing makes good sense and can give you the variety of a grocery produce department.

Sow fast-growing crops like radishes or lettuce in between melons or squash in the early summer, before the plants have started to spread out. Use quick-growing crops like vining beans to provide shade for plants that don't want too much summer sun, such as lettuce or quick-to-bolt cilantro.

Intercropping for shade: As the beans climb the poles, they'll shade the lettuce plants, which don't like heat.

Intercropping for space: Radishes will be harvested before the squash plants fill in the space.

MAINTAINING THE GARDEN

The rewards of regular weeding: a lettuce bed neat and healthy.

Mulching: pine needles make a neat-looking, spongy weed barrier. But remember—they make soil more acidic.

Weeds and Weeding

Weeds are unwanted, ever-present companions in the vegetable garden. There are a number of strategies to eradicate weeds, but none of these will ever bring permanent results. Starting seedlings indoors, and then transplanting, gives them a chance to get started before weeds move in. If weeds are a severe problem, planting in rows makes it easier to protect the seedlings. Mulching with impenetrable barriers or thick blankets of compost helps keep weeds down.

The Natural Way

Although careful attention to the labor of weeding seems unnecessary, consider the health of your household before reaching for an herbicide spray. None of the herbicide sprays are actually registered for use in vegetable gardens. Think of weeding as outside, exercise time. Take time to read up on possible health consequences from using chemicals on foods you plan to eat and share with your household.

Mulching

An organic mulch is one of the gardener's best tools, beneficial to plants and soil while saving time and effort. A thick, 4- to 6-inch mulch saves on watering and weeding chores, and conserves moisture by inhibiting evaporation from the soil. You will water less when your plants are well mulched. Weeding chores shrink because weeds have a hard time working their way up through a deep mulch.

Mulch also acts as an insulator, keeping the soil's temperature more consistent than if it were bare. Mulching in the fall, especially when applied in thick layers, helps protect some plants against early frost. In early spring, scrape mulch back from the base of the plants or off garden beds to allow the soil temperature to warm up. As the days and nights gradually stay warm, begin to build up the mulch again.

Although composted material is often used, mulch can also consist of partially decomposed pine needles, leaves or shredded or chipped tree bark and branches. Some gardeners like to add a deep layer of straw, but

WEEDING POINTERS

- **Hand pull weeds** before they go to seed.

- **Do not add** seed heads of weeds to the compost pile.

- **Start seeds early** and transplant.

- **Use thick layers** of newspapers, plastic sheeting or mulch as weed barriers.

- **Pull weeds** year-round.

For larger plants, such as these peppers, coarse wood bark makes a good mulch and pathway at the same time.

Newspaper (black and white only, not the glossy sections), laid 6-8 sheets deep, is a readily available mulch material. For looks and added protection, cover newspaper with bark or chips.

the layer must be at least 6 inches deep or you risk encouraging seeds to sprout in the straw. The deep layer of straw prevents the seeds from sowing in the soil. If some do sprout in the top layer of straw, it is a simple matter to dislodge them.

Mulches add nutrients to the soil as they break down. Pine needles and chipped bark add acidity to the soil as they break down. If you are mulching with these materials, check the pH regularly.

A weed-barrier fabric combined with pine needles helps keep these onion plants healthy, and a soaker hose supplies them with water at ground level.

Mulches can consist of six or more layers of newspaper (do not use the glossy paper sections) or cardboard; either will maintain a weedless garden path. These impenetrable mulches keep water away from plant roots, so place them away from the plant's stem unless they are on top of a drip irrigation system. After a couple of seasons, they will break down and you will have to reapply them. Melons, pumpkins and winter squash, which like warm soil temperatures, benefit from a black plastic mulch. If you do not have a drip system under the plastic, leave a place to water at the base of the plant.

Compost

With time, water and heat, plant material decomposes and melts into crumbly, sweet-smelling compost.

To make compost from a pile of grasses, leaves, straw, weeds or shredded bark is quite simple. Just go for a walk in the forest and dig down under a tree. You will come to a rich layer of natural compost made of leaves and plant debris which decomposed from the action of water and time breaking down the plant matter. So pile up your organic matter with a little soil and leave it set—you will eventually see the same compost that you found in the forest.

Slow Composting

It's easy to simply set up a large wire circle and pile in gar-

> **TIP** **LET NATURE DO IT**
>
> The much-touted bacterial additions you purchase to add to your compost pile are really not necessary. A compost pile will start to work without them, naturally.

> **TIP** **TURN OFTEN**
>
> A properly composted pile does not emit a bad odor. The key: Keep it turned and aerated, allowing nature's bacteria and enzymes to do their work.

No matter how simple it is, a compost heap is a valuable ally of any gardener.

den trimmings over a whole growing season. After letting it sit for a year or so, undo the wire, turn the compost, and shovel it onto your garden beds.

"Fast" Composting

Some gardeners prefer a faster-acting compost pile, with enough nitrogen to build up heat in the pile to kill any weed seedlings.

Layer the pile with fresh green grass clippings, dried leaves, sawdust, manure (either composted chicken manure or fresh cow manure) and weeds, wet kitchen trimmings (but no meat or dairy scraps), and more dried material.

Build up the layers, water it thoroughly, then cover the top with old rugs or burlap and let it sit. Decomposition builds up the heat in the pile, speeding the breakdown of the matter as well as destroying any stray seeds, particularly weed seeds. After several weeks, turn the compost pile to break up the layers, then cover again. Repeat the process, continuing to turn and let the pile sit. With this additional aeration, the pile quickly breaks down into compost.

There are also a number of commercially available composters in the marketplace which rotate to aerate the contents.

Sift compost to make a very fine, granular soil amendment. Or shovel compost directly over garden beds as partly decomposed mulch. Do not dig partly decomposed compost into garden beds, for as the compost continues to breakdown, it will deplete nitrogen from the soil.

Avoid the disappointment of broken stems by staking your tall plants. It's best to stake them when you plant them—you could damage the roots if you stake a mature plant.

COMPOST TIPS

Compost is decomposed vegetable matter. To make a compost pile, layer soil with leaves, twigs, fresh weeds (discard invasive plants such as morning glory, crabgrass and other noxious weeds), fresh manure, aged manure, wood ashes and any wet vegetable garbage from your kitchen.

Water each layer of the compost as you put it together. Assemble your material and make a pile at one time, or gather and add throughout the season, alternating different layers as you go. (See also page 27 for additional instructions.)

A couple of "don'ts": Don't add vegetable peels from purchased root crops like potatoes or carrots to your compost; some of these may carry soilborne diseases you do not want to introduce. To avoid attracting rodents, do not include any grains, animal fat, bones or meat scraps .

Staking

Many different garden plants require staking as they grow, either because they have a vining habit or because they become so heavy with their fruits that they threaten to fall over. Although vining plants can sprawl on the ground, those with tender fruit like tomatoes suffer from rot when the fruit comes in contact with the soil. In some cases when space is at a premium, training plants vertically conserves space, leaving room in the garden for a greater variety of plantings.

Put stakes in place when the plants are either transplanted to their site, or when they break

Training tomatoes this way gives the plants plenty of sunlight and room for fruit. It also gives you lots of elbow room for weeding, harvesting and other garden work.

out of the ground. Many a gardener has discovered the problem of trying to set up a tomato hoop when the plant is so large that limbs break off while trying to be moved inside the hoop.

Staking Methods

Teepees are easy to build and useful for a number of plants including beans, tomatoes and cucumbers. Woven wire attached to posts can make a long line of staking useful for beans, peas and other vines. Wire hoops are equally versatile. You can make

Teepees are time-tested space savers for a number of climbing vegetables. Tie the poles together with twine.

This sturdy trellising technique will support the weight of these fava beans even when they're full of meaty pods.

Peas don't need huge supports. Often you can get by with rustic twigs or small branches to support them.

Harvest your bounty daily to keep plants producing. And bring along your "gourd dog" to help!

them yourself from a length of woven wire or you can buy one of the commercial varieties that come in a number of different heights.

Remember that some plants climb by twining; others with tendrils grasp and twine around the support.

Twining plants twist around their support in only one direction depending upon the plant. If you try to twine a bean plant around a wire support in the wrong direction, you can break

off the tip. Some long, limber plants like melons need to be tied as they grow up their support. Melons, cucumbers and tiny icebox watermelons can be raised on a trellis or wire support. You must tie the fruit up in order to keep it from breaking its stem as it matures and grows larger and heavier. Some gardeners use hammocks made from cotton rags, mesh bags that oranges come in, or pantyhose.

Harvesting

Harvest your vegetables early in the day, before the heat saps them of their crispness. Make a daily pilgrimage to find vegetables before they grow too large.

Try to harvest squash when they are 4- to 6-inches long. In almost all cases, small vegetables are tender and sweet, while overgrown ones become woody and deteriorated. If you find zucchini that has grown huge while hidden under a leaf, stuff it with a savory filling or grate it for zucchini pancakes or bread. Picking stimulates a

continued harvest because plants not picked stop blooming, and consequently, stop producing.

Harvest herbs when the dew is just drying on them so that the leaves will be rich with the essential oil that gives them flavor. Edible flowers also benefit from early morning picking. If the leaves are dusty, swish the plants in a bucket of water, shake off the water and continue to process them.

Bring harvested vegetables, herbs and flowers inside to a cool place out of the sun until you have a chance to finish processing them.

Criss-crossing stakes helps bean plants by giving them more sunlight.

Proof that it's all worth it. You can't buy satisfaction like this at the store.

PESTS AND DISEASES

Tomato hornworms are caterpillars that look like they came from Mars just to eat your tomato leaves and fruit. Control them with trichogramma wasps, Bt or good old hand-picking.

These decorative woven covers let light and water in, but keep birds out.

These strawberry beds were kept insect-free with floating row covers.

Fill raised beds with disease-free soil and cover with protective screening or plastic.

Various creatures will compete with you for a share of your vegetable garden's bloom and harvest. Be cautious about using pesticides and herbicides on vegetables destined for meals. Pesticides can be absorbed from soil into the plant itself. If you choose to use pesticides and herbicides, read the directions thoroughly and follow them carefully. But a better plan would be to "go organic."

A tunnel of chicken wire, screening, or hardware cloth will keep birds, rabbits and curious cats away from crops.

Where deer threaten your garden, an 8-foot tall fence may be your best option. An alternative is a 5-foot fence with tall evergreens behind it; deer won't jump into an area they can't see into.

Control a swarm of plant-sucking aphids with insecticidal soaps or repeated sprays of water.

Organic Solutions

Although protecting your harvest by organic methods may be a little more labor intensive, a safe and productive garden for you and your family is a clear incentive.

- **Try the new series** of organic, soap-based pesticides that suffocate pests with fatty acids. These soaps are harmless to people and animals.

- **Look into** biological controls, such as lacewings and trichogramma wasps (very tiny and not like their larger stinging relatives), which attack plant pests without bothering you.

- **Consider using** *Bacillus thuringiensis* (Bt), a bacteria spray that kills caterpillars without leaving any harmful residue for humans.

Netting laid over bent pipes and anchored at the base will keep this new bed critter-free.

Viruses and fungi also attack plants, creating stunted, sometimes unusually-colored growth. As soon as you notice any small infected plants, pull them out and discard them in the garbage. Strip off infected leaves of larger plants, then watch the plants carefully for future signs of attack.

The best protection against soil-borne fungal diseases: Mixing generous quantities of organic compost into the soil, which encourages beneficial mi-crobes. If soil-borne diseases persist in your garden, consider growing less-resistant heirloom plants in containers, or raised planter beds filled with sterile potting mix. Discard the mix if disease strikes again.

GOOD CRITTERS

Here is a partial list of creatures that gobble up bugs harmful to your plants, or pollinate plants ... "good critters" you'll welcome into your garden.

Lady Bug Beetles: Eat mealybugs, scale, whiteflies and mites.

Lacewings: Eat aphids, mealybugs, scale, whiteflies and mites.

Syrphid Flies: Eat aphids, mealybugs, scale and whiteflies.

Soldier Beetles: Eat cutworms, gypsy moth larvae, cankerworms, snails and slugs.

Praying Mantis (can be purchased): Eats anything it can catch.

Wasps and Yellow Jackets: Eat small caterpillars.

Bees and Bumble Bees: Pollinate trees and plants.

Spiders: Eat anything that lands in their web.

Birds: Many nesting birds eat huge amounts of insects and caterpillars.

Honeybees and bumble bees are great pollinators. Don't use bug zappers if you care about keeping good-guy insects around.

Ladybugs are not only lucky, they dine on a host of small garden pests.

ORGANIC GARDENING

'Mammoth Russian' and other large sunflowers love regular feedings of fish emulsion, manure tea or other organic nutrients.

The word organic has become a puzzler for many home gardeners. Just what is an organic garden? Why should a home gardener be interested? Is this some faddish new gardening method, or is it something only dedicated purists pursue?

Organic gardening is a return to gardening the way it used to be practiced at home and by market gardeners up to World War II, before synthetic fertilizers and pesticides became widely available.

Why Organic

Organic gardening for the home gardener means growing fruits, vegetables and flowers without any synthetically produced fertilizers or pesticides. Gardeners have different reasons for choosing to garden organically. Everyone, especially parents raising food for their young children, wants homegrown fruits and vegetables to be nourishing, nutritious and free of pesticide residues.

Some gardeners choose organic gardening to make an ecological statement; others find organic gardening cost effective, because almost everything in the garden is recycled to manufacture copious quantities of compost—what some gardeners refer to as "black gold." Also, there are gardeners who swear by the improved flavor of their organically-grown produce. One blind taste-testing at Cornell University discovered tasters preferred organic tomatoes over those grown conventionally, finding them sweeter and less acidic.

Key: Compost

Converting your garden to organic methods is very simple, and begins with the soil. Most organic gardeners are fervent

A mouth-watering summer harvest of vegetables, all raised organically.

Celeriac (shown here), celery, carrots and other root vegetables will thrive in loose, humus-rich organic soil.

about their soil, working in lots of homemade or purchased organic compost (see pages 27-28), and using soil amendments made from natural ingredients such as rock phosphate, aged animal manure and even bat guano. Making compost is a bit like deciding on the best chili recipe—there are about as many opinions as there are cooks.

Whether you make your own or purchase organic compost, adding it to your soil is an essential part of organic gardening.

When you are planting, always work generous quantities of mature compost into the soil. The compost helps break up heavy soil, improving soil composition to allow plant roots to grow easily. At the same time compost absorbs nutrients from the soil.

Compost also fights disease. The good microbes from your decomposing compost fight for you and your plants against disease microbes in the soil.

Another comrade that works for you is the worm. Adding lots of compost to your soil and leaving off poisons encourages an underground community of worms. They weave their way through the soil, eat organic matter, add fertilizer and aerate the soil, all of which lets plant roots breathe.

FIVE RULES OF ORGANIC GARDENING

1. Use only natural products. Avoid synthetically produced pesticides and fertilizers.
2. Recycle your own garden clippings to make compost. Add generous amounts of compost to the soil when planting or use as a mulch around plantings.
3. If you are having a garden problem, find out exactly what is causing the problem and work to eradicate just *that* problem. *Target* the treatment.
4. Discriminate the good garden citizens from the bad. Some of the good bugs will consume your bad ones.
5. Encourage plant health through good garden habits, such as watering at proper times.

Choosing Plants

Buy first-quality plants, and check out their breeding. Look for plants that have been bred to be disease- and pest-resistant. In tomatoes, the initials VFN mean the plant has been hybridized to be resistant to verticillium wilt, fusarium and nematodes. Try different varieties in your garden and see what you can grow with a minimum of intervention. Banish fussy varieties that are susceptible to diseases.

Managing Pests and Disease

Learning the signs of insect or viral/bacterial destruction, and who or what caused them, can turn you into a backyard naturalist.

"Know before you spray" is one motto for organic gardeners. One of the side-pleasures of organic gardening is learning the way nature has balanced good bugs against

The tastiest eggplants come from organic growing methods. This is the dwarf variety 'Bambino'.

bad bugs. By not spraying, you can put the good critters to work for you. Most gardeners know that ladybugs find aphids as delicious as kindergartners do jelly beans. Even wasps and yellow-jackets work on your side by eating wiggly caterpillars that devour your plant's leaves.

You don't have to let these critters munch up your harvest. Organic gardeners feel that even though they are willing to share some of their harvest with the other denizens of the earth, there is a limit. Who wants to see their crops disappear? Having healthy plants is the first way to avoid the critters, because strong plants don't seem to attract pests the way weaker plants do.

Here are also some specific techniques and products for managing pests:

- **A jet of water** from your hose will wash off most sucking insects like aphids and leaf-hoppers. You may have to spray for several days in a row to really get rid of them.

- **Explore your garden** at night by flashlight to discover the slugs and snails and their midnight attacks of your lettuce patch. Pop them into a bag with a couple of tablespoons of salt and discard in the trash.

- **Rolled newspapers** become hotels for earwigs, collecting them nicely for you to shake out and stomp every morning.

- **Place pheromone traps** in your fruit trees just as the buds are opening, help keep the codling moth under control.

Organic gardening has a wonderful way of becoming a lifestyle choice. The subtle pleasures of studying ecology in your own garden, and encouraging the balance of nature to return, becomes a source of personal pride. The birds, bees and bugs become your partners in the harvest as you become a sensitive steward of your own plot of land.

A fall harvest of organically-grown vegetables and herbs sown in late summer: parsley, beets, carrots, radishes, fennel, savoy cabbage and chard.

TIP

ORGANIC FERTILIZERS

To supply the additional nutrition necessary for healthy plants, use organic fertilizers. Fish emulsion is a high-nitrogen fertilizer you dissolve into water and feed your plants as a liquid food. Although fish emulsion used to be incredibly smelly, manufacturers have now removed the bad odors. A number of other fertilizers (from kelp to bat guano) also work, so check your local nurseries to see what products they carry.

VEGETABLES IN CONTAINERS

A container-grown veggie garden will fit into the corner of a patio. This one includes peppers, chard, onions, tomatoes, cucumbers, celery, lettuce and endive.

Although most gardeners have in-ground space for vegetable gardening, growing vegetables in containers also makes sense.

Perhaps it's your only option, or the only area in your garden sunny enough for vegetables may be where there's a deck, patio or driveway. Perhaps your open land is so filled with tree roots that it would be difficult or impossible to cultivate for a garden. And there's an added benefit containers bring: Foiling those pesky gophers and other pests from munching on tender roots.

Mobility is also a plus, such as the ability to move a container under protection when frost threatens. When confined to a container, invasive plants (such as the mint family) cannot spread to become a weed in your garden.

Containers also let you grow plants you otherwise couldn't fit into your garden plan. Almost any plant can be grown in a container, although the harvest may not be as big and the size of the individual vegetables may be smaller. A consistent water and fertilizer program, and matching the size of the mature plant to the size of the con-

tainer, will go a long way in creating the right environment for a satisfying harvest.

Potting Mixes

Choosing the right potting soil mix for your container-grown vegetables is essential to produce healthy plants. It would be nice if you could fill pots with garden soil, but in almost all cases it is simply too heavy to promote good root growth and healthy plants. Garden soil alone, scooped into pots without careful attention to amendments, will probably not drain well enough to encourage your plants to thrive.

Garden shops and nurseries stock both soil-based mixes and soil-less mixes.

Soil-based Mixes

Soil-based mixes consist of sterilized soil along with amendments for texture. This soil has been sterilized to rid it of insect

Large raised beds can hold a lot of plants, and require less bending to tend. If you fill them with extra-rich soil, you can plant more intensively.

TOMATO BOUNTY

Variety is the spice of life, so they say. So why not plant a container to provide a rainbow of salad tomatoes? Try 'Sungold', 'Green Grape' and 'Sweet 100' for a gorgeous plate with a lively palette of colors. These varieties are indeterminate, so their foliage will fill any circular wire cage meant to fence them in. To ensure a continuing crop, regularly harvest the tomatoes. This is not likely to be much of a problem, for you will find family and guests clustered around the container helping themselves to the delicious bounty, right off the vine.

A series of hanging containers will work for cascading plants.

eggs, seeds and soil-based fungi. Some commercial soil-based mixes also have fertilizer added to the mix. Adding more fertilizer to this kind of mix may harm the delicate roots of seedlings, so read the label before you choose.

Soil-less Mixes

Soil-less mixes are made of peat mixed with sand, perlite or vermiculite. Perlite and vermiculite are minerals heated until they puff up as small particles that provide the proper texture and composition to a mix. Plants consistently perform well in soil-less mixes. These mixes provide no nutrition to the plants, so adding fertilizers is essential.

Drip Systems

The greatest challenge of container gardening is keeping pots consistently watered. A drip system on an automatic timer is perhaps the easiest and most reliable way to keep container plants well watered.

Depending upon how extensive a collection of pots you have, you can put together a simple, inexpensive drip system with parts bought from a nursery or hardware store. A manual system assembles quite easily, and can be hooked up to a garden hose which you turn on daily or several times a week, depending upon the weather. There are more elaborate automatic systems run by an electrical timer, which are not difficult to install if electricity is handy.

Proper Drainage Techniques

Almost every container-gardening book instructs the reader to add crockery to the bottom of a pot to improve drainage. This idea uses up all those broken terra-cotta bits most gardeners have lying around. Yet studies have shown that drainage is not improved, but actually impeded by this process. The layering of two different materials—the fine-grained potting mix on top and the crockery pieces on the bottom—actually slows down drainage.

Potting mix drains perfectly well by itself. After a few waterings, the soil mix will settle and not fall out, so you can simply leave the hole at the bottom of the container uncovered if you wish. Or cover the hole with a single piece of crockery or square of nylon screening, which has the added benefit of preventing snails or slugs from hiding inside the hole.

Wire containers hung outside your windows make handy, decorative containers for lettuce, edible flowers and herbs, but you'll have to pay attention to watering.

Peppers make nice ornamental container plants, and you can eat the ornaments. Give the plants frequent waterings and feedings.

Use smaller containers for smaller plants. Many chile peppers or herbs, for example, don't need huge containers.

Waxed milk cartons make inexpensive containers for seedlings. You can even grow small crops of herbs, lettuce or green onions in cartons if you're pinched for space.

Container Size

Knowing the specific growth rate and mature size of your plant helps you judge the size of the container it needs for good root development and healthy growth.

Most vegetables are fast growing, but lettuces need less root space than tomatoes because their mature size is much smaller. A container that is too small has limited space for root development and may stunt the growth of a fast-growing plant. Pumpkins and melons are so vigorous that stunting doesn't prevent them from flowering or fruiting, although production will be limited compared with a plant grown in the ground.

Invasive plants such as mint can be held in check by using pots. But you must root prune every year or so to keep the plant from becoming root bound, a situation where the roots circle inside the container and become matted and inefficient in aiding plant growth.

Containers

The shape of a pot affects the amount of room the roots have to grow. Square pots hold a larger volume of potting mix than round pots with sloping sides. The larger the volume of potting mix, the more room roots have to develop, resulting in a stronger, healthier plant. Some plants such as tomatoes have long roots, so pots that are deeper than they are wide fit their growing needs.

The simple rule of thumb is the larger the plant, the more extensive its root system and the larger the pot it will need. When growing seedlings, regu-larly check the drain hole of your containers to see if roots are beginning to show, indicating that the roots have begun to fill the container.

For maximum continued growth of plants—especially vegetable plants, which need continued, rapid development in order to produce their harvest—choose a large pot to minimize repotting chores.

One of the most useful containers for vegetable gardening is the half barrel. You can pur-

Containers should be large enough to let a plant develop a good root system.

Metal-ringed whiskey barrels are fine plant containers, but they hold a lot of soil. You'll need a dolly if you have to move them around.

MESCLUN MIX IN CONTAINERS

Use a potting soil mix that includes peat moss; this will help retain moisture. Place the containers right by your kitchen door for easy access. Use the largest containers you have: a 20- or 24-inch pot is just about right.

With three or four containers, you can plant one each week. After about thirty days, your first container will be ready to harvest. Make sure the containers don't get more than three or four hours

of direct sun, or the tender greens will burn. Seed the containers thickly and start your harvest by eating the thinnings.

Kale (shown here) and mesclun mix are both good container vegetables. Even an old washtub can be put to use if you punch drainage holes in the bottom.

Some bush cucumber varieties, for example 'Salad Bush' and 'Spacemaster', can be grown in containers.

chase these quite inexpensively, and they are large enough to grow a variety of crops that require deep root space or quantities of soil.

Have holes drilled in the bottom of the barrels to allow for drainage. Hammer in nails around the bottom edge of the iron hoops because if the barrel dries out, the hoop can slip, causing a misalignment of the stays.

Because the barrels look so large, do not be tempted to overcrowd any vining crops you plant, such as tomatoes, squash or pumpkins; no more than two plants in each barrel.

Mulching Containers

Mulching your containers creates a beneficial environment for potted plants. Covering the top of the soil with 2 to 3 inches of organic mulch helps retain moisture, keeps the roots cool and helps prevent weeds from germinating.

Finding the Right Spot

For summer vegetables, look for a location with at least six

hours of sun a day. But the specifics of the site will affect the true temperature the plant experiences.

Heat bouncing off a concrete pad can produce temperatures higher than the thermometer indicates. Direct afternoon sun can be too much for plants in containers, effectively baking their roots. Shade the bottom of the

container by surrounding it with other potted plants to keep the potting mix and plant roots cool.

Check your plants in containers frequently; if they are not thriving, try moving them to another spot with a different light pattern. Don't forget to dig down in the soil periodically to check that water is penetrating to the roots.

Containers are also a boon when you want to extend the harvest of cool season crops. Move plants such as radishes and lettuce into filtered shade, a situation better suited to their requirement for cooler temperatures. In hot weather, you may need to water at least twice a day. Mist the leaves to prevent the plants from wilting.

This container garden uses a stone wall to hold heat and boost the growth of warmth-loving cukes, tomatoes and beans.

Garden Plan

A WINTER VEGETABLE GARDEN

Although winter gardening does not succeed in climates with heavy snow, there are still a whole host of areas where a few hard frosts are as cold as it gets. Why hang up your trowel when a winter vegetable garden can provide your kitchen with fresh vegetables instead of limp produce flown in from faraway lands? The trick: Plant seeds in mid-summer. If you use transplants, you can delay planting until late summer.

In addition to using garden beds, you can also plant winter vegetables in containers that are easy to move to follow the winter sun in your garden. Planted in containers, you can bring tender lettuces inside or leave them under sheltering south-facing eaves when frost threatens.

The first step to replanting for winter harvest is to rework your garden beds. Take the time to turn over the soil in each bed, digging in plenty of organic compost and adding an applica-

Fiberglass or polyethylene tunnels can help you extend the growing season.

tion of complete fertilizer to replenish the nutrients used by your summer garden. If you have a problem with weeds, leave the beds unplanted for 2 weeks to let any weeds emerge, then hoe them out.

When and How to Plant

Direct seed vegetables for your winter garden around July 4 in shorter season climates, July 15 for longer season areas. If you are using good-sized transplants, you can wait until about September 1 in most areas.

This coldframe uses sliding doors for extra protection and insulation.

TIP   WINTER PREP

January's weather is perfect for updating your garden plan, reviewing last year's successes and the seeds unused from past gardens, and ordering new seeds.

Also take the time to clean and sharpen garden tools: rub the wooden handles of shovels and trowels with linseed oil; clean and oil all metal surfaces; use a sharpening file to work the edges of blades—of both cutting and digging tools—to a fine sharp edge.

Hardware stores often offer sharpening services if you prefer. You'll be amazed at the results come spring.

Use rowcover fabric, clear plastic sheets or hard plastic tents to make mini-hothouses for cold-sensitive plants.

FROST PROTECTION

Hardy and tender roughly distinguish how well a plant withstands cold. Hardy plants stand up to a certain amount of cold and are often described as hardy to a certain temperature—for example, "hardy to 32°F." Half-hardy plants will usually survive a cold spell, but may not survive extended cold weather. Tender plants may be

damaged by cold temperatures, and a freeze may kill them.

Protect plants against untimely frosts in a number of ways. Covering with polyfilament rowcover cloth can increase temperatures up to 3 or 4 degrees, which may mean the difference between life and death for your plants. A deep 12- to 15-inch mulch with

straw or leaves also provides insulation that can keep both roots and leaves from frost damage.

Rowcover fabric lets light in and can keep crops a few degrees warmer. It lasts for years too.

A simple styrofoam container with a clear top makes a portable greenhouse.

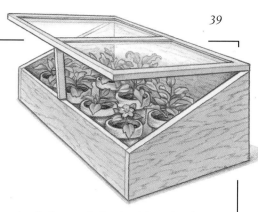

A window sash (no lead-based paint, please!), hinged to a slanted wooden frame makes an easy coldframe. Put fresh manure under the soil and you've got a hotbed (see p. 24).

What to Plant

Consider what types of winter vegetables are your favorites. Do you relish rutabagas and parsnips, or do you prefer salads with snips of tasty herbs? Fresh garden carrots and radishes are hits with kids and make great snacks, and they can be grown easily in containers. Mizuna can be used raw in salads, as a sandwich green or served Italian-style sautéed with olive oil and garlic.

Plant members of the onion family, from chives to scallions to garlic.

Perennial herbs planted in the fall will establish themselves in time to provide seasoning all winter long. Some of the sages die back to the roots when cold threatens. But parsley, thyme, oregano, rosemary and mint will continue to produce savory flavors throughout the winter months.

Try planting potatoes for a winter harvest. Depending on the frosts in your garden, this may be somewhat of a tricky endeavor, for an early frost will destroy the harvest. To avoid disaster, experiment with planting the tubers in a 2-foot by 4-foot raised bed underneath a south-facing roof eave. Smother the emerging plants with fallen leaves and garden compost. Continue to cover the plants as the foliage grows up through the leaves and compost; the potatoes will form under the mulch and the covering leaves may help protect your harvest.

If you don't have a lot of room for a vegetable garden, plant lettuce or kale in your flower borders to fill in for your outgoing summer annuals.

Don't give up when summer ends. In most areas winter gardens have the luxury of being watered by Mother Nature's rains, saving you the chore of watering. And you'll get garden-fresh produce when you want it most.

A Beautiful Look Too

Make your winter garden a cheery place to work during the gloomy, gray winter days. Try edging beds with the cheerful and edible blooms of nasturtiums, which will survive and bloom. Let Johnny jump-ups creep between plants, and sprinkle the little flowers on your salads. Create borders of parsley to give your winter garden spatial definition. Grow edible pod peas or sugar snap peas up your tomato cages; don't forget that the tender tendrils can be harvested and eaten, as well as the pods.

This trench greenhouse adds a warming effect even when the air is cold.

A Suggested List of Winter Plants

Here's a partial list of winter plants to try in your garden. In your garden diary, list the vegetables you tried this year, the season's temperatures from high to low, your successes and failures. Your winter garden diary will make an excellent guide when you start planning next year's garden.

Artichokes	Herbs: oregano, thyme,	Mizuna
Beets	rosemary, sage,	Potatoes
Brussels sprouts	spearmint, parsley	Radishes
Chinese greens	Horseradish	Scallions (green onions)
Chives	Kale, both green and	Shallots
Collards	decorative	Snap or edible pod peas
Garlic	Loose-leaf lettuce	Swiss chard
	Mâche	

Garden Plan

AN HEIRLOOM GARDEN

Heirloom beans come in almost all colors of the rainbow and have beautiful patterns. Some of them have been around for centuries. Oh yes—they're easy to grow and taste great too!

Heirloom tomatoes just cannot be beat for flavor. The large one here is the legendary 'Brandywine', the yellow is 'Rainbow' and the plum tomato is 'Jersey Devil'.

A book on French vegetables originally published in 1885 describes an astonishing diversity of vegetables. Organized alphabetically, the book starts with beans; every sort of bean is illustrated for the next 54 remarkable pages. Further on, melons consume 24 pages. Radishes are extensively discussed: the French turnip radish, the early white-tipped scarlet radish, the deep scarlet turnip radish, the small early white turnip radish and the small early yellow radish. There are intermediate or olive-shaped radishes and a bundle of other radishes until the last entry, the rat-tailed radish.

Plants like these give us a glimpse of our ancestry—a sense of those who gardened before us, digging their fingers into the warmth and richness of the soil to sow, grow and save seeds for next year's pleasure.

Sadly, many of these plants are lost to us, their seeds no longer available. But because of revived interest in open-pollinated plants, some of these heirloom plants have been rediscovered in seed banks and are being sold again today.

A Short History

The business of selling seeds started in the eighteenth century. In America, the Shakers were one of the first groups to package seeds for sale. At that time, individual groups or companies grew plants, improving the varieties by saving the seeds of the plants with the best characteristics.

Experimenting also accelerated at this time, with some cross-breeding taking place: taking pollen from one desirable plant and using it to pollinate another member of the same family. Sports—maverick plants that suddenly appear in a garden or field (the famous 'Mortgage Lifter' tomato is one)—were lucky accidents of nature which gardeners carefully preserved by saving the seeds every year. The growers always picked the strongest plants with the heaviest production for the seed parent.

Growing heirloom corn varieties, such as 'Country Gentleman', gives you unique flavors and colors.

TOP DOZEN HEIRLOOM PLANTS

Arugula
Beet 'Chioggia'
Bush bean 'Jacob's Cattle'
Carrot 'Oxheart'
Lettuce 'Red Oakleaf'
Lettuce 'Black-seeded Simpson'
Pole bean 'Kentucky Wonder' Snap
Runner bean 'Scarlet Emperor'
Squash 'Yellow Crookneck'
Sweet Corn 'Golden Bantam'
Tatsoi
Tomato 'Brandywine'

'Yellow Crookneck' is an open-pollinated summer squash that produces abundantly.

Hybridizing started early in the twentieth century, after Mendel's laws of genetics revolutionized the world of plant breeding. Plant breeders crossed plants in such a way they created "mules," or hybrids.

These hybrids produce seeds. But when planted, many of these seeds do not germinate, and those that do follow the traits of one parent, usually looking totally different from the original plant.

Hybridizing allowed the breeders to create plants with added disease resistance, improved yield, better shape and prettier blooms. Plants called

"F1 Hybrids" are the results of this process.

Open-Pollinated, Old-Fashioned Plants

The ritual of saving and storing seeds from open-pollinated plants takes us back to a simpler gardening time.

Some plants readily self-sow their seeds, dropping them carelessly to grow again the next year. But for those plants that don't reseed, the gardener's judicious harvesting, threshing, sorting and storing of the very best seeds neatly marks the end of the season with a promise of next year's harvest.

There is one caveat about growing old-fashioned plants. Heirloom plants have *not* been hybridized, and therefore do not have improved disease resistance and vigorous growth. In some cases, they need more coddling.

But with other heirlooms, you can plant

HYBRID OR OPEN-POLLINATED

Hybrid plants have been specially bred to produce particular characteristics. Because of their breeding, seeds do not duplicate the parent, but replicate grandparents or other breeding stock.

Seeds of open-pollinated plants will duplicate the parent exactly as long as they have not naturally cross-pollinated in the garden. Some plants (like lettuce and beans) are self-fertile and do not cross-pollinate. Others (like pumpkins and squash) will cross with other nearby plants, and subsequent generations of seed may not be true to the parents.

and then sit back and enjoy the results—their tough nature lets them take care of themselves. Careful cultivation and attention to matching the plant with your garden environment overcomes many difficulties.

Vegetable plants (tomatoes and potatoes, in particular) are susceptible to soil-borne diseases, so it's a good idea to rotate the planting in different beds each season. Additionally, working in copious quantities of organic compost (with the beneficial action of its microorganisms) can boost healthy growth of these heirloom plants.

Heirloom experts tell us that 'Jacob's Cattle' beans were originally grown by the Passamaquoddy Indians of Maine. They're a favorite choice for baked beans.

'Oxheart' is an open-pollinated heirloom carrot whose blocky shape makes it a good choice for heavier soils.

RAISED BED GARDENS

Raised beds aren't just functional. They can fit into almost any kind of garden style or location, even near the front entryway.

or soil. Raised beds can contain squash and other vining vegetable plants, which in a less formal garden would meander at will. Keeping a raised bed vegetable garden tidy is simplified as well. A rake or sweep of the paths, and everything looks quite decent.

Convenient and Functional

Raised beds at waist height are great for physically disabled gardeners, or for gardeners who experience pain or discomfort when kneeling. The higher beds

If you make the width of your beds twice the length of your reach, you'll be able to reach to the center from either side.

look quite dramatic with vining plants or with flowers draped down over the sides.

Design the beds to be narrow enough to be able to reach across from either side. Walking on the bed compacts the soil. Generally, the width should be no more than four feet across, but the length can be extended according to your preferences.

Confined in raised beds, the vegetable garden—sometimes deemed unlovely—looks neat and tidy. A raised bed with its loose soil, excellent soil composition and drainage, allows the roots to develop properly to support strong, healthy plants.

Paths in between the raised beds can be grass, gravel, paved

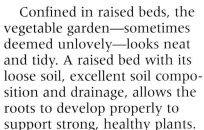

Raised beds fit in with patio areas and workspaces. Note all the vertical elements in this garden, making it feel like a room.

Wide edges on raised beds make good sitting areas. They make it a lot easier to work the beds and reach the harvest too.

Raised beds are good for starting young plants or for single-crop plantings.

Placing a potting shed amid raised beds gives you a ready work site for transplanting, mixing plant food, beating the sun or updating your journal.

Construction

Beds must be sturdy, for the weight of the soil and the effect of watering can quickly destroy a shoddily built bed. Construct raised beds of long-lasting wood like redwood or cedar, recycled plastic or even railroad ties or pressure-treated wood. Research has been done into whether creosote in railroad ties or arsenic used in the pressure-treated wood leach into the surrounding soil in quantities harmful to humans. The verdict indicates such usage is safe, but your better bet may be to use untreated wood. Enclose the bed's sides and bottom with long-lasting hardware cloth to deter destructive gophers and moles.

Although the raised bed contained by wood is handsome and practical, mounded beds have the same effect. There aren't the crisp lines of the wood-edged beds, but mounds are still quite handsome and functional.

Soil

In both types of raised beds, work the soil by adding compost and soil amendments for maximum fertility, optimum soil composition and improved drainage. This improves the quality of both heavy clay and sandy soils.

Check the beds with a pH indicator after you have worked the soil and watered it thoroughly so you know exactly what the pH measures in each bed. Most vegetables grow best in soil with a pH between 6.0 and 7.0.

Small-space gardens can still be productive with raised beds. Paths let you get equipment and supplies to the beds.

A youngster can have his or her own garden in a single raised bed.

PLANNING RAISED BEDS

Plan your garden beds or mounds according to how plants grow. Melons, squash and pumpkins benefit from a circular raised mound with generous quantities of compost and fertilizers worked into the soil to provide the fertility necessary to grow their large fruits. Grow climbing plants like tomatoes and cucumbers in long beds with wire climbing supports or large 3-foot diameter wire circles for them to clamber up. Plant corn in blocks at least four rows wide for the best pollination. Grow lettuces in raised beds or mounds in light shade during the hot summer months.

AN EDIBLE LANDSCAPE GARDEN

When vegetables were mostly grown at home, large vegetable gardens existed by themselves, with neat rows of each crop. Now, with space at a premium, adding edibles to your landscape makes great and delicious sense. The term *edible landscaping* refers to integrating your vegetable garden into the ornamental landscape. Perennial borders can be edged with parsley or lettuce, while artichokes (some to harvest and some to bloom with their bright purple heads) can anchor the back of a bed. Pansies, with their edible blooms, can be grown in drifts around beds of lettuce.

Other possibilities include red-stalked chard, bright green heads of cabbage and a parterre (see definition on page 45) of

Mixing herbs, flowers and vegetables in your planting plan is a tenet of landscape gardening. Purple basil, lettuce, marigolds, onions and parsley make this garden a salad ready for the picking.

lettuces interlocked by an edging of thyme.

Making a Plan

The first step in accomplishing this look is to forget about the old-fashioned vegetable garden. Throw out the rule books that dictate flowers and vegetables should be separated and that vegetables should be in neat, symmetrical rows.

A perennial border always needs annuals to fill in while the plants are maturing, so pop

in vegetable plants instead, then harvest them before the space is required. The bright,

Edible pansies combine with salad greens in this attractive bed.

This formal hedge contains abundant plantings of tomatoes and flowers.

bronze color and interesting leaf texture of deer's tongue or oakleaf lettuce add interest to any garden. Johnny-jump-ups are small self-sowing plants with tiny pansy-like flowers that surprise dinner guests when the flowers appear tossed among the lettuce greens in salads.

Herbs are also useful landscape plants. Thyme can edge beds and rosemary can be sheared as a hedge. Use society garlic (with its variegated green-and-white leaves and edible, onion-flavored pink blossoms) to splash bright spots of color along a border.

Larger vining plants, such as pumpkins and squash, are more difficult to integrate because they sprawl everywhere. But melons and cucumbers can be trellised, leaving space below for flowers, herbs or a border of flowering chives. Planting corn with the pumpkins and squash conserves space. A west-facing slope makes an excellent spill-way for winter squash.

Once you begin to experiment with mingling vegetables and flowers, you will discover that you can make your borders more interesting and more colorful. Sowing thickly, harvesting trimmings and thinning as the plants grow keeps the flower border from looking bare. Successive planting after harvest continues the kitchen's bounty and preserves the garden's look.

Here, asparagus and marigolds combine to make a front yard garden look good. The asparagus needs to grow its leafy fronds after harvest in order to give food to the roots for next year's crop.

"It's springtime," says this bed of daffodils, romaine lettuce and primroses.

 TIP

DEFINITION: PARTERRE

A parterre is an old landscaping device that uses neatly hedged rectangles to surround beds of vegetables. Invented by the French in the 18th century, the Chateau Villandry in Loire, France, continues to make good use of parterres.

◖ CHAPTER 3 ◗
VEGETABLES A TO Z

I t's fine to talk about gardening strategies—how to make a vegetable garden plan, how to work the soil and make it rich, how to manage pests such as weeds and insect problems.

All that is important. But sooner or later it's time to get your hands in the dirt. That starts with making selections on putting the right plants in the right places at the right times. From that point to harvesting the vegetables you've grown, success depends on understanding the habits and characteristics of the plant you're working with.

That's what this section, "Vegetables A to Z," is all about. We've included everything from artichokes to zucchini. More importantly, each vegetable is covered in detail, revealing the whats, wheres, hows and whys of growing that particular vegetable plant successfully.

There's much more to vegetable gardening than just throwing some seedlings or seeds into the ground. With the proper knowledge and understanding—found here—you can watch your harvest grow and grow, and enjoy the fruits (and vegetables!) of your labor even more.

HOW TO USE THIS SECTION

This section, "Vegetables A to Z," presents the key facts, insights and gardening strategies you need to know to grow vegetables successfully.

Is this plant truly an annual, or just grown as one? What kind of soil does it prefer? Will I be able to grow it in containers or in beds? Can I plant in mounds, or should I create rows? Does it need full sun, or will it tolerate some shade? What about watering requirements? How do I propagate it? When do I plant or trans-

plant? What are harvesting tips that will help me pick my produce with the correct technique and at the right time? What are storage guidelines?

This chapter presents the answers to all these questions, and more. Just turn to the vegetable you're interested in. At a glance, the keys (explained on this page) will give you the basics you need to know about growing that vegetable. Then let the words and pictures guide you to complete vegetable growing success.

Light Requirements

Full Sun. Prefers sun most of the day.

Light Shade. Prefers more shade than sun.

Full Shade. Prefers shade most or all of the time.

Edible Parts of Plants

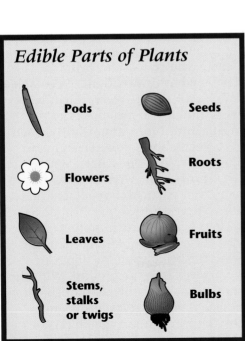

Pods

Seeds

Flowers

Roots

Leaves

Fruits

Stems, stalks or twigs

Bulbs

Background and History

Description

Planting, Soil and Growing Instructions

Varieties You Can Choose From

Propagation Methods

Troubleshooting Tips

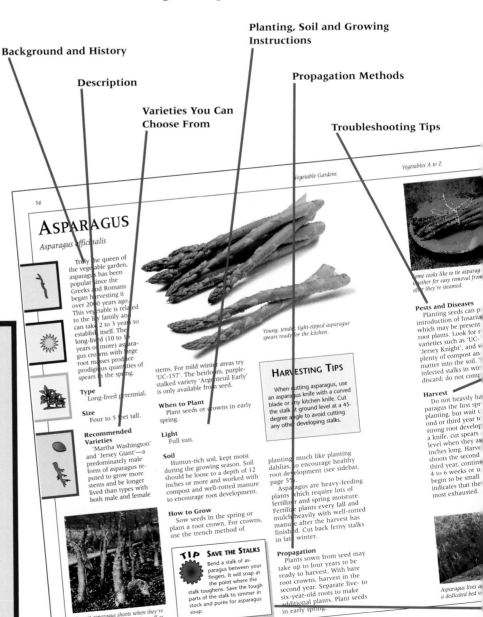

54

ASPARAGUS
Asparagus officinalis

Truly the queen of the vegetable garden, asparagus has been popular since the Greeks and Romans began harvesting it over 2000 years ago. This vegetable is related to the lily family and can take 2 to 3 years to establish itself. The long-lived (10 to 15 years or more) asparagus crowns with large root masses produce prodigious quantities of spears in the spring.

Type
Long-lived perennial.

Size
Four to 5 feet tall.

Recommended Varieties
'Martha Washington' and 'Jersey Giant'—a predominately male form of asparagus reputed to grow more stems and be longer lived than types with both male and female

stems. For mild winter areas try 'UC-157'. The heirloom, purple-stalked variety 'Argenteuil Early' is only available from seed.

When to Plant
Plant seeds or crowns in early spring.

Light
Full sun.

Soil
Humus-rich soil, kept moist during the growing season. Soil should be loose and worked to a depth of 12 inches or more and well-rotted manure to encourage root development.

How to Grow
Sow seeds in the spring or plant a root crown. For crowns, use the trench method of

Young, tender, tight-tipped asparagus spears ready for the kitchen.

HARVESTING TIPS

When cutting asparagus, use an asparagus knife with a curved blade or any kitchen knife. Cut the stalk at ground level at a 45-degree angle to avoid cutting any other developing stalks.

planting much like planting dahlias, to encourage healthy root development (see sidebar, page 55).

Asparagus are heavy-feeding plants which require lots of fertilizer and spring moisture. Fertilize plants every fall and mulch heavily with well-rotted manure after the harvest has finished. Cut back ferny stalks in late winter.

Propagation
Plants sown from seed may take up to four years to be ready to harvest. With bare root crowns, harvest in the second year. Separate five- to six-year-old roots to make additional plants. Plant seeds in early spring.

TIP SAVE THE STALKS
Bend a stalk of asparagus between your fingers. It will snap at the point where the stalk toughens. Save the tough parts of the stalk to simmer in stock and purée for asparagus soup.

Harvest asparagus shoots when they're five to eight inches tall. Cut them off at an angle.

Some cooks like to tie asparagus together for easy removal from after they're steamed.

Pests and Diseases
Planting seeds can p... introduction of fusarium which may be present... root plants. Look for r... varieties such as 'UC-... 'Jersey Knight', and w... plenty of compost and... matter into the soil. T... infected stalks in win... discard; do not comp...

Harvest
Do not heavily ha... paragus the first spr... planting, but wait ti... ond or third year to... strong root develop... a knife, cut spears... level when they are... inches long. Harve... shoots the second... third year, contin... 4 to 6 weeks or u... begin to be small... indicates that the... most exhausted.

Asparagus lives at... a dedicated bed w...

Propagation

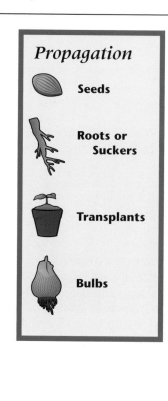

Seeds

Roots or Suckers

Transplants

Bulbs

Zone 1:	Below -50°F
Zone 2:	-50° to -40°
Zone 3:	-40° to -30°
Zone 4:	-30° to -20°
Zone 5:	-20° to -10°
Zone 6:	-10° to 0°
Zone 7:	0° to 10°
Zone 8:	10° to 20°
Zone 9:	20° to 30°
Zone 10:	30° to 40°
Zone 11:	Above 40°

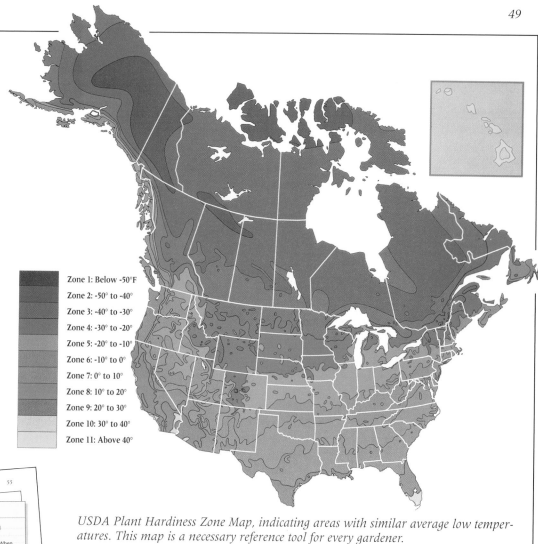

USDA Plant Hardiness Zone Map, indicating areas with similar average low temperatures. This map is a necessary reference tool for every gardener.

Bonus Recipe Ideas

55

Asparagus with Herbed Butter

4 pounds of freshly harvested asparagus, trimmed, washed and drained
4 tablespoons herbed butter (see page 149)

Add the herbed butter to a large sauté pan over medium-low heat. When the butter has melted, add the asparagus, cover and cook. Shake occasionally and continue to cook until the asparagus is tender, about 4 to 6 minutes depending upon the size of the spears.

Serve immediately. Serves 4 as a side dish.

Asparagus "berries" are colorful and fit in nicely in the autumn edible landscape.

TRENCH METHOD OF PLANTING

Dig a hole 12 inches deep and 18 inches wide. Place a rich mixture of soil and compost in the bottom of the hole. Mound up a triangle of soil at the bottom of the hole and place a crown on a mound, arranging the roots around. Set the crowns 3 to 5 inches below the level of the soil. Space plants 1 foot apart in trenches, and allow 3 feet between rows. As the shoots grow up through the soil, continue to cover them until soil level is reached. Every fall, cut off any shoots and mulch the bed with compost and dried manure.

Storage
Harvest and cook immediately for the sweetest flavor. If that is not possible, place stems upright in warm water and refrigerate 1 to 2 days only.

In the Kitchen
Asparagus is delectable quickly sautéed in butter and herbs. Wrap steamed stalks with prosciutto to serve as hors d'oeuvres. You can stir-fry, grill, bake, pickle or steam asparagus.

Other Uses
Although usually grown in a separate bed, the decorative value of the plants makes them eligible for placement in the back of perennial beds.

Slice asparagus spears on the diagonal to open up more of the tender inside.

Harvesting Guidelines

Detailed Methods and Instructions

How to Store

Using Your Garden's Bounty

Many Other Great Tips

Annual, Biennial or Perennial

Annual. Germinates, flowers, sets seed and dies in one season.

Biennial. Germinates in spring, produces leaves, but doesn't bloom until the following spring or summer. Many vegetables are biennials that are grown as annuals in the garden.

Perennial. Continues to grow and bloom each year.

ARTICHOKES

A cross-section of an artichoke shows its tender inner leaves, the fibrous "choke," and the tender heart.

Globe Artichokes
Cynara scolymus

Italian immigrants introduced globe artichokes to America. The blossom heads of artichokes can be pickled, sautéed, boiled, baked, frittered or sliced for raw salads. Actually a thistle, globe artichokes are totally unrelated to Jerusalem artichokes and perform best in regions with a mild winter climate. Gardeners in cold winter areas have luck treating this tender perennial as an annual.

The tiny side blossoms can be eaten whole when young and tender. As the blossom heads mature, the prickly choke—or more descriptively, the hay—must be removed; only the bottom (heart) and the meaty base of the leaves are tender enough to eat.

Type
Biennial in mild-winter climates, annual in cold-winter areas.

Size
Four to 5 feet tall and spreading, with sucker plants around the base.

Recommended Varieties
'Green Globe' and 'Imperial Star'—claimed as the easiest to grow from seed—are the usual varieties. Gourmet gardeners have discovered 'Violetto', a purple blossomed variety with piercing thorns reputed to be hardier than 'Green Globe'. Many Northern gardeners have also had success with 'Grande Beurre'.

When to Plant
Fall in mild-winter climates, early spring in cold-winter areas.

Light
Full sun in cool coastal areas, part shade in hot summer areas.

Soil
Humus-rich soil. Keep moist during the growing season.

How to Grow
In mild winter areas, after harvesting the spring crop, cut the plant back to the base to encourage fresh growth and a second blossoming flush. In cold winter areas without snow, cut plants back again in the fall and cover them with 4 to 6 inches of straw, compost or manure. Replace the plants every 3 to 4 years for maximum production. In the summer, heavily mulch plants to keep roots cool. For fall harvest, continue to irrigate all summer. Artichokes can be drought tolerant but they will not bloom without watering.

For snowy winter areas, treat artichokes as an annual. Start new plants every year from seed and set them out in

These artichoke heads are ready for harvest while their leaves are still tight.

An artichoke flower, close up.

early spring—when it's still cold—as long as the temperature doesn't fall below 25°F.

Propagation

You can grow artichokes from seed. Or separate the suckers around the base of the mother plant in late fall or early spring. If planted early in the fall, you can expect a crop the following spring in mild-weather areas.

Pests and Diseases

Gophers eat the roots, aphids may attack young growth. Plant the roots in wire baskets to thwart the gophers, and wash off the aphids with repeated jets of water.

Harvest

Cut off the central blossom when the head is large but the overlapping leaves are still tightly closed. Leave about 1 inch of stem on the bottom. Allow side shoots to develop and harvest the smaller heads similarly. Once the heads start to open, the artichoke toughens.

Storage

Store in plastic bags in the refrigerator produce drawer for up to 1 week.

Grilled Artichokes

Artichokes grill magnificently. Their smoky flavor adds something extra to pizza, or tastes sublime when gobbled with a dip of freshly made aïoli. Here's how to grill them:

Prepare the artichokes by peeling off the outer leaves until you reach the more tender, pale green-yellow leaves. Trim ½ inch from the top leaves and trim the stem to about ½ inch long. Cut the artichokes in half and rub with lemon juice to prevent discoloration. Using a melon scooper, take out the choke, or thistle, just above the heart of the artichoke.

Drop the prepared artichokes into boiling water to which you have added 2 tablespoons of vinegar. Cook for 15 to 20 minutes, depending on the size of the artichokes, or until the artichokes are tender. Drain thoroughly in a colander. Brush olive oil over the surface of the artichokes and grill on both sides until browned.

Serves 1.

In the Kitchen

Boil or steam whole artichokes until the base of the leaves are tender. Tiny side stalk artichokes can be trimmed and boiled; or pickle them and eat them whole.

Other Uses

Use as an annual or perennial landscape plant. Harvesting only the large center artichoke lets the side blossoms develop their purple thistle blooms.

Artichokes can create a stunning effect in the landscape.

Cardoon
Cynara cardunculus

Although this plant looks very similar to the artichoke, it is grown for the flavor of its stems, which taste like a combination of artichoke and celery. During the 1831 to 1835 voyage of the *HMS Beagle*, Charles Darwin noted that the cardoon had aggressively naturalized across the South American pampas. In mild winter areas of Northern California, the cardoon has repeated this feat. But in most gardens, the cardoon must be treated as an annual. Sow seeds in early spring and harvest the fleshy stalks in early summer. Tying the leaves up and piling straw around the base blanches the heart, much like celery, for an early fall harvest. The noted horticulturist L. H. Bailey suggests the root is also edible, but this is never mentioned in cookbooks.

Type
Perennial grown as an annual in cold winter climates.

Size
Four to 6 feet tall.

Recommended Varieties
Cardoon seeds are available but hard to find. Search for them in catalogs offering unusual plants (see Sources, page 154). Varieties are usually unnamed.

When to Plant
Early spring in cold weather climates, late fall in mild winter climates.

Light
Full sun.

Soil
Rich, moist humus.

How to Grow
Prefers cool, moist growing conditions similar to artichokes.

In short season climates, start seeds indoors 6 weeks before the last frost. Keep well watered during the growing season. To blanch (whiten and tenderize) cardoon, tie up the leaves over the heart at the end of the growing season. Pile up straw around the base and cover with dirt to seal out light. Harvest after about 3 weeks.

Propagation
By seed, or dig up roots and winter in a cool, dark place, then plant again in spring after the last chance of frost. Separate side shoots and plant individually.

Cardoon is a lovely plant, but it takes some space—it can spread to six feet wide.

To reach their largest growth capacity, these young cardoon plants will have to be transplanted to between 2 and 4 feet apart.

Pests and Diseases

Roots may be eaten by gophers. Tender shoots can be attacked by aphids; wash off with a strong jet of water.

Harvest

Sixty days. Cut young tender stalks early in the growing season or harvest the whole blanched hearts later in summer.

Storage

Refrigerate after harvesting and use within two or three days.

In the Kitchen

Cook young, tender stalks in spring and early summer, hearts later in the summer. Avoid the older hollow stalks which are tough and stringy and have little flesh to cook. Boil the stalks in acidulated water (water that has a small amount of lemon juice or vinegar added to it) until tender, then string like celery. Finish the dish by baking in a cream sauce or braising alongside a baked chicken.

Other Uses

Cardoon is a large and elegant plant in the landscape or flower border, grown not only for its striking foliage but its beautiful blossoms as well.

In cooler regions, start cardoon inside and transplant it when danger of frost has passed.

Grilled Cardoon

4 pounds cardoon
4 garlic cloves
1 bay leaf
¼ cup olive oil
Salt and pepper to taste
Lemon juice or white wine vinegar

Prepare the cardoon; trim off the leaves and cut the pieces into 4-inch long strips. Because cardoon blackens when exposed to air, drop the trimmed cardoon immediately into water acidulated with lemon juice or white wine vinegar. Remove the cardoon from the acidulated water after a couple minutes, then poach in fresh water with 2 teaspoons of salt for 35 to 40 minutes or until the pieces are tender. Remove them from the water and when they are cool, peel the strings from the cardoons as you would with celery.

Crush the garlic cloves with the back of a knife and place them in a non-reactive bowl large enough to hold the cardoon. Add the bay leaf and the olive oil. Let the cardoon marinate in the olive oil mixture for 1 to 2 hours or overnight, turning occasionally in the marinade.

When you are ready to cook the cardoons, remove them from the olive oil and drain briefly. Grill them over a moderate heat until golden brown.

Serves 4 as a side dish.

ASPARAGUS

Asparagus officinalis

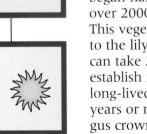

Young, tender, tight-tipped asparagus spears ready for the kitchen.

Truly the queen of the vegetable garden, asparagus has been popular since the Greeks and Romans began harvesting it over 2000 years ago. This vegetable is related to the lily family and can take 2 to 3 years to establish itself. The long-lived (10 to 15 years or more) asparagus crowns with large root masses produce prodigious quantities of spears in the spring.

Type

Long-lived perennial.

Size

Four to 5 feet tall.

Recommended Varieties

'Martha Washington' and 'Jersey Giant'—a predominately male form of asparagus reputed to grow more stems and be longer lived than types with both male and female

stems. For mild winter areas try 'UC-157'. The heirloom, purple-stalked variety 'Argenteuil Early' is only available from seed.

When to Plant

Plant seeds or crowns in early spring.

Light

Full sun.

Soil

Humus-rich soil, kept moist during the growing season. Soil should be loose to a depth of 12 inches or more and worked with compost and well-rotted manure to encourage root development.

How to Grow

Sow seeds in the spring or plant a root crown. For crowns, use the trench method of

Harvest asparagus shoots when they're five to eight inches tall. Cut them off at an angle.

TIP SAVE THE STALKS

Bend a stalk of asparagus between your fingers. It will snap at the point where the stalk toughens. Save the tough parts of the stalk to simmer in stock and purée for asparagus soup.

HARVESTING TIP

When cutting asparagus, use an asparagus knife with a curved blade or any kitchen knife. Cut the stalk at ground level at a 45-degree angle to avoid cutting any other developing stalks.

planting, much like planting dahlias, to encourage healthy root development (see sidebar, page 55).

Asparagus are heavy-feeding plants which require lots of fertilizer and spring moisture. Fertilize plants every fall and mulch heavily with well-rotted manure after the harvest has finished. Cut back ferny stalks in late winter to make room for new shoots.

Propagation

Plants sown from seed may take up to four years to be ready to harvest. With bare root crowns, harvest in the second year. Separate five- to six-year-old roots to make additional plants. Plant seeds in early spring.

Some cooks like to tie asparagus spears together for easy removal from the pot after they're steamed.

Asparagus with Herbed Butter

4 pounds of freshly harvested asparagus, trimmed, washed and drained
4 tablespoons herbed butter (see page 149)

Add the herbed butter to a large sauté pan over medium-low heat. When the butter has melted, add the asparagus, cover and cook. Shake occasionally and continue to cook until the asparagus is tender, about 4 to 6 minutes, depending upon the size of the spears.

Serve immediately. Serves 4 as a side dish.

Pests and Diseases

Planting seeds can prevent introduction of fusarium wilt which may be present on bare-root plants. Look for resistant varieties such as 'UC-157' and 'Jersey Knight', and work plenty of compost and organic matter into the soil. Trim off infected stalks in winter and discard; do not compost.

Harvest

Do not heavily harvest asparagus the first spring after planting, but wait until the second or third year to allow strong root development. Using a knife, cut spears at the ground level when they are 5 to 8 inches long. Harvest only a few shoots the second year. The third year, continue cutting for 4 to 6 weeks or until the spears begin to be small and thin. This indicates that the roots are almost exhausted.

Asparagus "berries" are colorful and fit nicely in the autumn edible landscape.

Storage

Harvest and cook immediately for the sweetest flavor. If that is not possible, place stems upright in warm water and refrigerate 1 to 2 days only.

In the Kitchen

Asparagus is delectable quickly sautéed in butter and herbs. Wrap steamed stalks with prosciutto to serve as hors d'oeuvres. You can stir-fry, grill, bake, pickle or steam asparagus.

Other Uses

Although usually grown in a separate bed, the decorative value of the plants makes them eligible for placement in the back of perennial beds.

TRENCH METHOD OF PLANTING

Dig a hole 12 inches deep and 18 inches wide. Place a rich mixture of soil and compost in the bottom of the hole. Mound up a triangle of soil at the bottom of the hole and place a crown on a mound, arranging the roots around. Set the crowns 3 to 5 inches below the level of the soil. Space plants 1 foot apart in trenches, and allow 3 feet between rows. As the shoots grow up through the soil, continue to cover them until soil level is reached. Every fall, cut off any shoots and mulch the bed with compost and dried manure.

Asparagus lives a long time, so put it in a dedicated bed with nutrient-rich soil.

Slice asparagus spears on the diagonal to open up more of the tender inside.

BEANS

Phaseolus vulgaris

Fresh homegrown green beans are a season-long kitchen favorite.

Golden wax beans are beautiful additions to any garden.

As common as they are now, it may seem strange that beans are comparatively new on the European world's culinary menu. Christopher Columbus lists them in his log, along with the exotic fruits and vegetables—the real gold as it turns out—that he brought back to Spain. Beans, along with tomatoes and potatoes, had been in cultivation for centuries in the "New World." Today beans rank only second to grains as a worldwide source of vegetable protein.

For the gardener's convenience, there are beans that grow on compact, low bushes or others that stretch up poles or teepees with showers of beans hanging down. Plant a variety in your garden so you never become bored. Try flat beans, round beans, purple beans or yellow beans. Enjoy shelling beans in bright rainbow colors from cranberry red to pink and white.

Value beans for the versatility of their culinary forms. Cook tender string beans by steaming, or sauté them quickly in herbs and olive oil to just-crunchy and sweet. Pop shell beans out of their pods to cook quickly like peas for a high-protein meal. Leave older pods on the vine until yellow and shriveled, then shuck the thoroughly dried beans and save them to reconstitute for soups and stews.

Type

Annual except for runner beans which grow as tender perennials in mild winter climates.

Fava beans like rich, well-drained soil. Set plants six to eight inches apart.

Utilize garden space better by going vertical. Pole beans will produce more than bush beans in the same space.

TIP

GARDEN HELPERS

Besides being delicious in the kitchen, beans are beneficial in the garden. The roots of beans, like other members of the legume family, are nitrogen-fixing; this improves the soil for whatever crop you plant next.

Size

Bush beans are 2 to 3 feet tall, pole beans can climb 8 to 12 feet tall.

Recommended Varieties

Numbers of bean varieties are staggering with every size, shape and color imaginable. 'Fortex' and 'Blue Lake' round beans are classic pole beans long grown for

Yard-long or asparagus beans are fun to grow and have a delicious flavor.

The colorful vines of "Scarlet Runner" beans can reach 12 feet high.

their prolific harvest and flavor. The skinny, toothpick bean 'Verite'—a filet bean—makes fabulous pickles or a tasty side dish. Don't forget yellow beans such as 'Goldmarie' or the bush type 'Goldkist'. The purple podded beans, although they look lovely on the vine, turn green with cooking. Try 'Purple Queen', a bush bean, or 'Trionfo', a pole type.

The unusual foot-long asparagus bean (so called because of its flavor), also known as the yard-long bean (*Vigna unguiculata*, subsp. *Sesquipedalis*), is eaten pod-and-all like a snap bean. Fava or broad beans (*Vicia faba*) are beloved in Italy, eaten for the fresh seeds. Try 'Romano', bush beans eaten as fresh beans or left to mature for green shelling beans. Eat lima or butter beans (*Phaseolus lunatus*) when young as snap beans, or let them mature into rich-tasting beans, consumed fresh or dried.

Runner beans (*Phaseolus coccineus*) provide decorative flowers in bright red colors beloved by hummingbirds. 'Painted Lady' shows off a two-tone blossom. Some varieties can be eaten young as snap beans or left to fatten for the marbled-pink, dried beans. Eat soybeans (*Glycine max*) when young as snap beans or let them mature to produce beans.

For something unusual, try the black soybean, 'Black Jet'.

The heirloom dried bean 'Jacob's Cattle', with its splashes of bright white and red color, may make you become a bean collector.

Purple pod beans come in bush and pole forms. Their color turns green when the pods are steamed.

When to Plant

When the soil warms in the spring and night temperatures do not fall below 50°F.

Light

Full sun.

Soil

Humus-rich soil, kept moist during the growing season. Do not over fertilize. Keep the pH about 5.5 to 6.5.

How to Grow

Plant according to whether the beans are bush beans or pole beans.

Plant bush beans in rows; space plants 6 inches apart, and leave 18 inches between rows. Set up a staking system for pole beans and plant beans 6 inches apart.

Keep the soil moist but not soggy. After the seedlings are about 6 inches high, mulch them with 3 inches of organic compost. Beans are shallow rooted and require plenty of daily moisture.

Propagation

Seeds or transplants. Do not soak beans before planting.

Pests and Diseases

Soil borne diseases can infect beans. To avoid diseases, water at the base of the plant rather than overhead. At the end of the season, cut off the plant but leave the roots in the soil to save the nitrogen nodules. Rotate crop location from year to year. Plant hybrid, disease resistant varieties if soil disease is a problem in your garden.

Harvest

Snap beans mature in 50 to 65 days; fresh shell beans, 70 to 80 days; dried beans, 85 to 105 days.

Harvest snap beans when pods are slim and tender, before they swell with seeds. Harvest fresh shell beans when the pods plump from seeds. Let dry beans hang on the vines until the pods turn yellow and shrivel; then cut off the roots and lift up the whole plant and hang it upside down in a warm, dark place. Shell the beans individually or place the whole dried bush in a cloth sack and beat to break the beans out of the pods.

Pick green beans every day to assure a continuous supply of tender beans. Larger pods become woody and fibrous.

Fava or broad beans prefer cooler weather.

BACK TO BASICS: DRIED BEANS

Baked beans were once a staple when meat was reserved for feast days and when a bean pot celebrated Sunday dinners.

With contemporary lifestyles, dried beans seem time-consuming to prepare. That's why more and more dried bean cultivars disappear from garden catalogs every year, even though beans provide superb nutrition and are high in protein and fiber.

It is too bad that they are often sadly lacking in our diet. Dried beans provide a great deal of practicality, for they store well in the pantry and are always ready to make a great meal. Soaking them overnight in the refrigerator makes them ready to cook up the next day.

Dried beans will last a long time in dry, airtight containers.

Storage

Fresh snap beans and shell beans freeze well. Store dried beans in an airtight, glass jar and examine them periodically. Beans with tiny round holes in them, or dust in the bottom of the jar, indicates an infestation of tiny beetles: Empty out the beans, sort the good from the riddled and reseal. Place the jar in the freezer for five days to kill any remaining beetles.

In the Kitchen

Eat just-picked green beans raw with dips, pickled, quickly sautéed or briefly steamed. Above all, don't boil green beans:

Much of the sweet flavor will disappear into the water.

Sauté shell beans until just soft, then toss with olive oil and herbs. Freshly harvested and shelled flageolet beans are the traditional accompaniment to roast leg of lamb. Dried beans make chili, stews and any imaginable number of vegetarian dishes; they are high in vitamins, minerals and protein.

Other Uses

Colonial Americans dried beans in the pod by stringing up the whole bean when it had swelled with seeds. These dried bean pods, known as leather britches, were then long-cooked in stews.

French-cut green beans need very little cooking time.

Pick young snap beans before the seeds begin to swell.

Traditional Beans

The old-time bean pot is cooked in a hole in the ground. Wood or charcoal burns on a bed of sand in a deep, 2- to 3-foot hole. A covered pot filled with softened/soaked beans, liquid and seasonings and sealed with aluminum foil is lowered into the hole. Sand covers the pot, which is left to simmer for 24 hours. When pulled out, the beans are mellow, fragrant and delicious.

BEETS

Beta vulgaris

Earthy beets come in many colors, shapes and sizes.

Besides being a colorful description of blushing, the term "beet red" also describes the bright red spots of beet juice used as rouge by 19th century courtesans.

The beet actually started out as a plant grown for its greens, its root ignored. The Romans are credited for developing the root to edible stage, and the conquering Roman armies introduced beets around Europe. Brought to America by the colonists, the red beet was thought to be the best eating. White and yellow beets were also grown, as well as a whole family of giant beets, called mangels, used to feed stock in the winter.

Beets can be left in the ground through winter in mild-winter gardens but when the weather turns warm, they bolt and become woody. The tops, cooked as fresh greens when the plants are young, do not have the stronger flavor of the mature beets.

Type
Biennial, usually grown as an annual.

Size
Tops grow 8 to 12 inches tall, depending upon variety.

Recommended Varieties
Easily grown in the cool gardens of spring and fall. The red globe is only one of a number of delicious varieties. Beets are not boring! Shock your dinner guests by serving 'Chioggia' with spinning pink and white rings of color, or 'Golden' for duck-yellow beets and 'Albina Verduna', a white beet. 'Formona' grows long like a carrot. 'Red Ace' matures quite early, but for long winter storing try 'Winter Keeper'. Worth hunting for is the heirloom variety 'MacGregor's Favorite', eaten for its edible purple foliage and not the roots.

> **TIP** **NATURAL FOOD COLORING**
> Older cookbooks suggest cooking a small red beet in with applesauce to turn the sauce a delicate pink tone.

When to Plant
Two weeks before the last frost until early summer; mid-summer for fall harvest and over-wintering.

Light
Full sun.

Soil
Well-worked, humus-rich soil kept moist during the growing

Mangels or forage beets are primarily grown for livestock, but they can be people food when picked young.

'Chioggia' is an Italian heirloom beet. The fresh roots have bright rings of color.

Cold Borscht

Here's the standard recipe for cold borscht. Although the taste is an acquired one, borscht is a tradition that has lived on for may centuries. It originated in Central and Eastern Europe, a traditionally Jewish technique for making something festive from the beets that came from the cold, rocky ground.

10 large beets, peeled and grated
$2^{1}/_{2}$ quarts water
1 onion, minced
$2^{1}/_{2}$ teaspoons salt

2 tablespoons sugar
$^{1}/_{4}$ cup lemon juice
2 eggs
1 cup sour cream

Combine the beets, water, onion and salt in a saucepan. Bring to a boil and cook over low heat for 1 hour. Add sugar and lemon juice. Cook 10 minutes more and season to taste.

Beat the eggs in a bowl. Gradually add them to the soup, stirring steadily to prevent curdling. Chill well. Serve before dinner, or serve with boiled potatoes at dinner. Whenever you eat borscht, garnish it with sour cream.

Makes about 2 quarts.

Beets have yellow and even white cultivars. Do they taste the same as red beets? Try 'em and see!

season. Keep the pH near neutral, from 6.5 to 6.8, to avoid scab on the beets' surface.

How to Grow

Plant seeds ½ inch deep in well-worked soil. Thin plants when they are 3 to 5 inches high, spacing plants 3 to 4 inches apart. Thinning is essential to good root growth. Keep plants moist to avoid bolting or woodiness.

Propagation

Seeds or transplants. To save the seed, plants must grow as biennials.

'Crosby Egyptian' is a red heirloom variety with a sweet flavor.

Pests and Diseases

Leaf miners sometimes attack the leaves—pick and destroy injured leaves. Gophers may destroy roots, so plant seeds in a wire-lined planting bed if this could be a problem.

Harvest

55 to 80 days. Use the thinnings as greens or in a fresh salad. Harvest tops as needed, leaving some of the tops on each plant. To extend the harvest, pick 2-inch-wide baby beets and let others develop to mature size. Fall harvests are sweeter after one or two frosts.

Storage

Beets keep well in a dark, cool space.

In the Kitchen

Eat beets raw, grate in salads or cube to pickle. Roasted beets taste great, and pickled beets have long accompanied antipasto plates. Borscht, the Russian beet soup, warms up the coldest winter day; when served chilled, it cools down the hottest day. Yellow and white beets don't bleed like the red ones do.

Other Uses

Try drying beets for chips. French-fried beet chips are another unusual but delicious way to eat beets.

You can pick beets at any time, but they're tenderest when they're one to two inches across.

These freshly picked beets are ready for boiling, baking or pickling.

CABBAGE FAMILY

Brassica spp.

The cabbage family includes a major portion of cool-weather crops including Brussels sprouts, broccoli, cabbage, cauliflower, kale and collards, kohlrabi, bok choy, broccoli raab, mustard greens and turnips. All these important vegetables are thought to descend from the wild cabbage, *Brassica oleracea*, a native of the Middle East. Spreading both to the east and to the west, cabbage family members became important foods in many cultures. Whether fresh or pickled, dried or stir-fried, cabbage family members serve as a vegetable staple around the world.

Broccoli and Broccoli Raab
Brassica oleracea

If there is one favorite vegetable prescribed by doctors, it may well be broccoli: filled with vitamins, minerals and phytonutrients, all cancer-fighting agents. From the gardener's point of view, broccoli ranks high for minimal effort and exceedingly delicious results. In addition to the common green-headed type are other varieties such as 'Romanesco' (with chartreuse-yellow conical heads) and broccoli raab, the sprouting broccoli, grown for the rich taste of the stalk and not the flower head.

Type
Grown as annuals.

Size
Twelve to 18 inches.

Recommended Varieties
Look for broccoli varieties that produce plenty of side shoots, for an almost endless supply for the kitchen. Try 'Saga' which can take some summer heat; the heirloom variety, 'Early Purple Sprouting', a purple-headed type; 'Early Green', which likes cool weather for spring planting; and 'Waltham', a good fall variety.

'Calabrese' or 'Minaret' are Romanesco types of broccoli; both offer a long harvest season, and the chartreuse flower heads look gorgeous in a bed of annual or perennial flowers.

'Di Rapa,' a broccoli raab, grows quickly in the cool seasons.

When to Plant
Early in spring, or mid-summer for a fall harvest.

Light
Full sun in coastal climate areas, part shade in warm weather areas when planted in summer.

Soil
Humus-rich soil, kept moist during the growing season. Work in plenty of fertilizer.

How to Grow
Transplant seedlings or sow directly early in spring. Thin to 12 inches apart for the best growth. Keep broccoli well-weeded and watered for the best growth. Side-fertilize with a liquid, high-nitrogen fertilizer once a month.

Propagation
By seed, or transplant young seedlings.

Pests and Diseases
Enclose young plants with floating row covers to keep root maggots and cabbage moths

Most broccoli varieties will keep producing side shoots after the main head has been cut.

'Rapine' is one reliable variety of broccoli raab.

Broccoli plants need a goodly amount of moisture. Use soaker hoses or drip systems to deliver and inch or two of water per week.

away. Spray the soil with Bt when you see cabbage moths fluttering around plants; they lay eggs in the soil which hatch into voracious caterpillars.

Harvest

Hybrid broccoli, 60 to 102 days; 'Romanesco' broccoli, 95 to 102 days; broccoli raab, 45 to 60 days, depending upon variety and garden climate.

Harvest broccoli when the center head is large but tightly bunched. Cut the big, center head off low and at a slant to encourage the side shoots to grow little heads for continued harvest. Keep harvesting the side shoots before they start to blossom or the plant will halt production.

For broccoli raab, harvest the tender shoots when they are about 8 to 10 inches tall. They will quickly regrow for two or three additional harvests.

Storage

Store in a plastic bag in the vegetable drawer for no longer than 2 or 3 days.

In the Kitchen

As a fine point in the preparation, use a vegetable peeler to trim off the tough exterior of the broccoli stalk. Steam or sauté broccoli briefly; cook through but not to the point of mush. Serve warm or cold in soups or in salads, or baked as a gratin. Broccoli pairs well with curry-spiced sauces, either hot or cold.

Other Uses

Lightly steamed just past the point of rawness and then cooled, broccoli makes a fine scoop for dips.

Don't overcook broccoli. A light steaming retains the bright green color while giving the best flavor and nutrition.

Sautéed Broccoli Raab

4 cups broccoli raab, sliced in 2-inch pieces
2 garlic cloves, finely chopped
2 tablespoons olive oil
1 tablespoon capers
¼ teaspoon red pepper flakes or chili powder
Salt and pepper to taste
2 tablespoons Parmesan, Asiago or hard Jack cheese, grated.

In a medium-sized sauté pan, heat the oil until it is moderately warm. Turn in the broccoli raab and toss in the oil. Continue to cook for another 4 minutes, stirring constantly. Add the capers, red pepper flakes and garlic. Cook for 1 minute. Add the salt and pepper to taste. Turn the broccoli onto a warmed serving platter and lightly top with the grated cheese.
Serves 4.

*Broccoli raab (*Brassica rapa*) is grown for its leaves and small florets, instead of a head.*

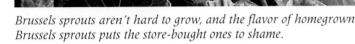

Brussels sprouts aren't hard to grow, and the flavor of homegrown Brussels sprouts puts the store-bought ones to shame.

Brussels Sprouts
Brassica oleracea

This *Brassica* was developed in Northern Europe somewhere before the sixteenth century. The plant we know was bred from a wild, kale-like relative. Brussels sprouts are one of those pivotal vegetables that inspire gardeners. Simply taste freshly harvested, sweet sprouts out of your garden and you are converted. Homegrown sprouts are not at all like the dried up, bitter types found in the grocery stores. Brussels sprouts sweeten up even more with a few light frosts in the fall.

Type

Biennial, grown as a slow maturing annual, exceedingly hardy. Withstands fall frosts.

Size

Usually 2 to 4 feet tall depending upon variety.

Recommended Varieties

If you are growing sprouts for the first time, try the hybrids such as 'JBS 596', 'Valiant' or 'Prince Marvel'. The heirloom varieties 'Bedford Fillbasket', and 'Rubine Red' (a plant with jewels of red sprouts) are worth trying after you get familiar growing Brussels sprouts.

When to Plant

Late spring or midsummer for a fall and early winter harvest, respectively.

Light

Full sun in coastal climate areas, some part shade in warm weather areas.

Soil

Humus-rich soil, kept moist during the growing season. Work in plenty of high-nitrogen fertilizers. Soil pH should be above 6.0.

How to Grow

Brussels sprouts take from 85 to 125 days to harvest, depending upon the variety and the climate.

In most climates, transplant seedlings or direct-sow in midsummer (earlier in short season growing areas), planting seeds 1/4 inch deep. Thin plants to 18 inches apart. Remove big leaves after sprouts form.

Plants will continue to grow despite frosts, and the sprouts will sweeten. In mild-winter areas, mulch heavily and continue to harvest through the winter. Side-fertilize with high-nitrogen liquid fertilizer once a month.

TIP **THE REAL THING**

Bitter, overcooked, store-bought Brussels sprouts instantly offend the palette. Instead grill, sauté or roast your garden-fresh Brussels sprouts to win over an audience which may have, in the past, experienced distasteful, mushy sprouts.

Don't change your breakfast drink, but Brussels sprouts contain more vitamin C than oranges.

Sprouts that are about an inch wide are very tender.

Wilted Brussels Sprouts Salad

This is a deliciously different way to wake up the wonderful flavors of Brussels sprouts. However, it only works with the freshest, home-grown sprouts. Market-purchased produce will be too bitter for such a delicate treatment.

4 cups Brussels sprouts
2 tablespoons olive oil
2 slices bacon, diced into small pieces
1 onion, finely chopped
1 teaspoon balsamic vinegar
Salt and pepper to taste

With a paring knife, carefully cut out the core of the Brussels sprout and separate the leaves. In a medium-size sauté pan, add the olive oil and heat until the oil is warmed. Add the bacon. Stirring constantly, cook for 1 minute. Add the chopped onion and continue to stir, cooking until the onion is just starting to turn golden and translucent—about 4 more minutes. Remove the pan from the heat. Turn in the leaves of the Brussels sprouts. Then, with two forks, toss the leaves of the sprouts in the hot oil and bacon mixture. Add the balsamic vinegar, then salt and pepper to taste. Toss again and serve.

Serves 4 as a side dish.

Propagation

By seed, or transplant young seedlings.

Pests and Diseases

Enclose young plants with floating row covers to keep root maggots and moths away. Spray the soil with Bt when you see cabbage moths fluttering around plants.

Harvest

85 to 125 days, depending upon variety.

Best harvested after several frosts have sweetened the sprouts' flavor. Simply break off the sprouts, starting at the bottom of the stalk, when they are 1 to 2 inches wide and firm.

To harvest the whole stalk at once, prepare early. Pinch off the top of the stalk when the bottom sprouts are about ¾ inch wide. In about a month, all the sprouts should be equally ready for harvest; then cut off stalk at the bottom.

Storage

Before the ground freezes firm, pull up the whole plant by the roots and place in a cool dark place. Brussels sprouts will keep on the stalk for two weeks or so.

In the Kitchen

Try cutting out the central core and separating the leaves of the sprouts. Sauté the leaves in a small amount of butter, stirring continuously for 4 to 6 minutes. Add a bit of cream if you want, add salt and pepper and serve.

Shock your dinner guests by blanching the fresh sprouts and then grilling them on skewers well brushed with a garlic-flavored olive oil. Wrapped in prosciutto and grilled until fragrant with a smoky flavor, they become bite-sized hors d'oeuvres.

Other Uses

Brussels sprouts freeze well. You can pickle them fiery-hot like the Korean pickle *kimchi,* or use in sweet pickle flavorings.

After buds form, pull the lower leaves to help the tiny heads or sprouts develop. The effect is oddly ornamental, too.

Cabbage, Chinese Cabbage
Brassica spp.

Cabbage has been in the kitchen since 400 B.C. In the fifteenth and sixteenth centuries, cabbage was the primary winter leafy vegetable throughout Europe. From there it traveled to the newly settled American colonies.

Vilmorin-Andrieux, a vegetable chronicler and author of *The Vegetable Garden* (published in France in 1885), described pages and pages of cabbages, from drumhead types—with a flattened head poetically compared to a drum—to common or curly-leafed types. With names like 'Late St. John's Day', 'Early Dutch', 'Schweinfurt', or 'Fumel', cabbages were held in high esteem as a reliable food source.

Cabbage lasted in the root cellar when other green-leafed plants disappeared over the long European winter. Save for the cabbage, this "vegetable fast" was broken only when the warmth of spring stirred up the dandelions and other potherbs.

The savoy cabbages, a loose-head type, did not keep as long, but many varieties were grown for their fine flavor. Now added to the European cabbages are a very tender-leafed type variously called napa or Chinese cabbage. These can be cooked in stir-fry or used as salad greens, particularly when teamed with citrus.

Because cabbages are held in high esteem in many different cuisines, there are hundreds and hundreds of delicious recipes. Stuffing a whole savoy cabbage, rolling up individual leaves around a savory filling, long-simmered soup and crunchy fresh coleslaw are only a few entries in cabbage's long and storied culinary heritage.

Type
Biennial, grown as an annual.

Size
Depends upon variety from small, 6-inch heads to giant types 12 to 16 inches in diameter.

Recommended Varieties
Why waste garden space growing big, pale-tasting, boring green cabbages? Instead, make room for the red cabbages such as 'Ruby Ball' and the rich-tasting

Red, green, napa, savoy and Chinese cabbages all have their place in the healthful kitchen.

Savoy cabbages like 'Chieftain'. You can plant the more tender-leafed Chinese cabbages such as 'Blues' in early spring.

Savoy cabbages have wrinkled leaves. They're favored by many cooks who say that savoys have the best flavor.

Chinese cabbage comes in different shapes. The tightness and density of the leaves varies too. 'Orange Queen' is one good Chinese cabbage cultivar.

TIP
CABBAGE COVER-UP

Some people find the smell of cooking cabbage to be objectionable. Try covering the lid of the pan in a clean cloth that has been immersed in a vinegar-water solution and wrung out. The vinegar dissipates the cabbage smell.

Both heirlooms, 'Early Flat Dutch' yields heads up to seven pounds; 'Late Flat Dutch' needs three or four more weeks and can give 10- to 12-pound heads.

When to Plant

Cabbages are particularly geared to the season, so plant early, midseason, and late varieties to provide cabbage to your kitchen all year round.

Harvest cabbage heads when they become firm. Use a sharp knife to make a clean cut.

Light

Full sun in coastal climate areas, some part shade in warm weather areas.

Soil

Humus-rich soil, kept moist during the growing season. Work in plenty of fertilizer.

How to Grow

Transplant seedlings or direct-sow early in spring. Thin according to type of plant. Sow again in mid-summer for a fall harvest.

Propagation

By seed or seedling.

Pests and Diseases

Enclose young plants with floating row covers to keep root maggots away. Spray with Bt when you see cabbage moths fluttering around plants.

Harvest

Harvest the entire head when it is large and firm, but before it begins to split. Fall's cool weather lets heads grow longer

without splitting. For optimal winter storage, cut off heads when green and still growing.

Storage

Cabbages keep well. Store them in a cool dark place or the crisper drawer of the refrigerator for months. If outer leaves brown from storage, peel them off before cooking.

In the Kitchen

Use cabbage in almost any possible fashion from pickling and fermenting for sauerkraut to grating fresh for coleslaw.

Other Uses

Use poached cabbage leaves to roll up delectable fillings.

Red cabbages make nice color contrasts in the garden.

Chinese Cabbage Salad

This fresh-tasting salad falls delightfully between "coleslaw" and "greens." Its flavors are satisfying and go well with grilled meats.

1 napa cabbage, leaves sliced very thin
2 scallions, thinly sliced
2 tablespoons finely chopped cilantro
1 clove garlic, finely chopped

3 tablespoons peanut oil
1 teaspoon rice wine vinegar
1 teaspoon soy sauce
1-inch knob of ginger
Salt and pepper to taste

¼ cup toasted peanuts, coarsely chopped, for topping

In a salad bowl, toss the cabbage, scallions and cilantro. In a small bowl, stir together the garlic, peanut oil, rice wine vinegar and soy sauce. Grate the ginger and squeeze the grated pieces in your hand, letting the juice drip into the bowl. Discard the ginger. Whisk together the vinaigrette and toss with the cabbage. Season to taste with the salt and pepper. Sprinkle the peanuts over the top and serve.

Serves 4 as a salad.

Cauliflowers come in white, light orange, light green and red forms.

flavored 'Violetto di Sicilia'. Seeds of the heirloom 'Purple Cap' may be hard to find.

When to Plant
Early in spring or mid-summer for a fall harvest.

Light
Full sun in coastal climate areas, some part shade in warm weather areas.

Soil
Humus-rich soil, kept moist during the growing season and with a pH of 6.5 or higher to prevent clubroot, a fungal disease. Work in fertilizer before planting.

How to Grow
Transplant seedlings or direct sow ¼ inch deep in early spring. Keep rows 18 inches apart and leave 24 inches between plants. Sow again in mid-summer for a fall harvest. When transplanting, keep seedlings well-watered to prevent

Cauliflower
Brassica oleracea, var. *botrytis*
Some people know cauliflower only as the white, broccoli-like stem used to scoop into dips at parties. But cauliflower has a longer and wider culinary application. It was so appreciated at the court of Louis XV that the royal chefs named a cauliflower soup Creme du Barry, after the king's mistress. Samuel Johnson, the noted 18th century English writer, thought it quite the most delectable "flower" in the garden.

Cauliflower grows successfully only in cool weather. The head of the flower (called the curd) may begin to separate as it ages but never bursts into bloom. Plant

breeders have developed different varieties to grow all through the year, but growing cauliflower in the fall brings the best results. Choose the self-blanching types to save yourself the trouble of tying up the leaves to keep the cauliflower white. Or grow the green- or red-headed types.

Type
Biennial, grown as an annual.

Size
From 16 inches 24 inches wide depending upon variety.

Recommended Varieties
Due to the tendency of cauliflower to bolt in the spring, stick to fall types. Try the self-blanching hybrid 'Fremont', 'Violet Queen' or the fine-

This creamy white head fits in nicely to an ornamental bed.

Coconut Milk Curry Cauliflower Soup

This savory curry soup is just the thing for cold winter days. Increase the amount of curry to your own taste. If you wish, sprinkle toasted, finely-chopped peanuts over the top just before serving.

2 tablespoons olive oil
2 large onions, coarsely chopped
2 garlic cloves, coarsely chopped
1 carrot, diced
1 cauliflower
4 cups chicken stock
1-inch knob of ginger
2 tablespoons curry powder
1 can coconut milk
2 tablespoons finely chopped cilantro
Salt and freshly ground pepper to taste
2 onions, thinly sliced
1 tablespoon olive oil

Pour the oil into a medium-sized, heavy-bottomed pot. When the oil is warm, add the chopped onions, garlic and carrot. Stir over medium heat until the onions start to look translucent but before they begin to brown. Break the cauliflower into small pieces and add to the pot. Add the chicken stock and ginger.

In a small bowl, mix the curry powder with a spoonful of stock until it is smooth and without lumps. Stir the curry mixture into the soup. Cover the pot and simmer for 30 minutes or until the cauliflower is tender.

Add the coconut milk and the cilantro. Adjust the seasonings with salt and pepper. Keep on low heat while the onions cook.

Place the oil in a small sauté pan over medium heat and add the sliced onions. Cook and stir constantly until the onions turn a medium brown color, about 10 to 15 minutes. Serve a tablespoon of caramelized onions on top of each serving of soup.

Serves 4.

stress, which could affect head formation.

If heads are not self-blanching —the leaves naturally enclose the heads—then tie outer leaves to surround heads when you first see the small white curd. Check progress of the curd regularly, and retie as needed.

Propagation

Seed or transplant young seedlings.

Pests and Diseases

Enclose young plants with floating row covers to keep root maggots away. Spray with Bt when cabbage moths hatch forth and start fluttering about.

Harvest

Pick when cauliflower heads are large and firm, and just beginning to separate slightly. Fall's cool weather lets heads stay longer without splitting.

Storage

Store in a cool dark place or the crisper of the refrigerator for no more than 1 week.

In the Kitchen

Cauliflower tastes milder than broccoli, yet offers a whiff of cabbage. Like rice, its subtle flavor lets it shine in any number of dishes. It serves well as a foil for stronger accents.

Cauliflower stars in a vegetarian curry served with side dishes of grated cucumber and toasted peanuts. Try the soup Creme du Barry, updating it by substituting coconut milk and topping with caramelized onions (see above recipe).

Is it a green cauliflower? No, it's actually a cousin, broccoli 'Romanesco'.

CARROTS

Daucus carota var. *sativus*

The carrot, native to Afghanistan, was originally a skinny-rooted vegetable that was gradually improved through breeding. Soon it migrated west and became a part of Greek and Roman cuisine. When it traveled from Europe to the New World with the American colonists, it escaped and became the wildflower Queen Anne's lace. If you pull the wildflower up, you can see its white, carrot-like edible roots just like the original carrot.

The carrot itself is the swollen base of the taproot. There are quick-growing globe varieties as well as the traditional long, skinny types. Because you want the roots to grow quickly and with ease, soil composition is the most important part of preparing the carrot bed.

Carrots are one of the best ways to convert young children to eating their vegetables; a sweet, round carrot pulled out of the ground and rinsed makes even a vegetable resister an instant convert. One carrot a day supplies all the Vitamin A you need.

Type
Biennial, grown as an annual.

Size
Roots can grow 10 inches long while tops stay about 10 to 12 inches tall.

Several types of carrots: in general, the long, slim 'Danvers' and 'Imperator' types like looser soils; the blocky, blunt or round types are suited for heavier soils.

Recommended Varieties
Plant a variety of carrots in your garden. Try 'Chantenay', a reliable 7-inch long tapered carrot. 'Planet' or 'Thumbelina' are good round types with sweet flavor. 'Danvers' is a delicious heirloom variety.

When to Plant
From early spring to mid-summer for a fall harvest.

Carrots have a place in any garden and in every cuisine.

Young carrots lightly steamed and glazed, with walnuts.

Light

Full sun.

Soil

Sandy soil rich in humus, kept moist during the growing season. Because these are root crops, the soil must be well-worked 6 to 12 inches deep to a fine composition, without lumps or rocks. Do not apply fresh manure; that can cause roots to fork.

How to Grow

Sow the seeds in early spring about ½ inch deep. They take about 2 to 3 weeks to germinate, so sow thickly and keep the soil crust moist: This keeps the seeds from drying out and allows them to break through. Some gardeners mix radish seeds with carrot seeds both to locate the row and as an easy way to help thin the carrots.

Lay soaked newspaper or burlap over the planted seeds to help keep them moist. Check regularly after the first 10 days and remove the topping at the first sign of seedlings. For best results, thin carrots to 2 inches apart.

Propagation

By seed sown directly in the soil. Carrots do not transplant.

Pests and Diseases

Blight and root maggots can strike carrots. Crop rotation should control any problems.

Harvest

Leave carrots in the ground until they color deeply. Then they will taste the sweetest. The little ball types are ready in 50 to 60 days, while longer carrots take about 70 days to mature. If left in the ground too long, carrots may split.

Don't remove all the soil right at harvest. Clean your carrots just before using them.

Harvest carrots whenever they're large enough to use. Remove all but about 2 inches of the tops so roots stay firm.

Storage

The garden bed is the best storage place for carrots. Twist or cut off tops of carrots after harvesting. (The tops draw up moisture from the roots, making them shrivel.) Store carrots in a plastic bag in the refrigerator crisper or a cool, dark place. For a large crop, store them in a cool root cellar in moist sawdust.

In the Kitchen

Use raw as healthy chips for dips or in salads, grated, in baked goods and chopped in stews or soups.

The smaller cultivars grow well in containers. This one is 'Short n' Sweet'.

Carrot, Apple and Lemon Marmalade

This marmalade will have all your breakfast guests puzzling over its ingredients. The bright range of colors and the wonderful taste make it well worth the effort.

1 pound carrots (about 3 large) peeled and diced
1 pound apples (about 3 large) peeled, cored and diced
1 lemon, juiced and the peel sliced into slivers
3 cups sugar
2 tablespoons dark rum (optional)

Just cover the carrots and apples with water in a saucepan and cook until tender, about 15 minutes. Drain them thoroughly, saving 1 cup of liquid. Return the carrots, apples and liquid to the saucepan. Add the lemon juice, peel and sugar. Cook over medium heat, stirring constantly, until the syrup reaches jelly stage—when drops of syrup dripped on a saucer hold shape for an instant before breaking. Take the saucepan off the heat. Stir in the rum. Ladle into hot, sterilized jars, leaving ¼ inch headroom. Clean the rims with a damp cloth, put the lids in place and tighten down. Invert the jars for a few minutes, then return to upright. Let cool completely. Check the seals, label and store in a cool, dark place.

Makes 2 pints.

CELERY AND CELERIAC

Apium graveolens

Celery is a graceful plant that needs humusy soil, full sun and lots of water.

'Smooth Prague' (shown here) and the closely related 'Giant Prague' are two tasty heirloom varieties of celeriac.

Recommended Varieties

Choices of celery and celeriac are quite limited. Try the old celery favorite 'Ventura' and celeriacs 'Brilliant' or the milder 'Mentor'. One English variety of celery called 'Pink Plume' footnotes that it has pink-tinged stalks. This type must be related to the heirloom 'Giant Red', also rare and difficult to locate.

When to Plant

In the spring, start seeds inside as they are extremely small. Use a heating mat underneath seedling pots to keep potting mix temperature between 55°F and 85°F. Seedlings can take 10 to 12 weeks to mature. Plant seedlings outside when the soil warms in

Instead of one plant with a savory root and delicious stalks, here are two plants that provide one or the other.

The familiar celery, when grown at home, has an exceedingly sweet flavor whether blanched or not. The root, celeriac, grows to the size of a softball, but you may want to harvest it at a smaller size. This vegetable provides a delicious white meat in the fall. When cooked, celeriac can be chopped and tossed in mayonnaise or

vinaigrette for a salad, or pureed for a cream soup. German cooks shred raw celeriac for a cole slaw type of salad.

Type

Biennial, grown as an annual, although celery can be grown as a biennial in mild-winter gardens.

Size

Celery grows to 16 inches tall, celeriac, about 12 inches tall.

Store celery in the refrigerator until you're ready to use it. If stalks get limp, cut a bit off the ends and place them in ice water for a while. They should crispen up again.

STALK HISTORY

Sadly, Dr. Brown's Celery Elixir, a 19th-century carbonated drink flavored with crushed celery seeds, is no longer available. Celery has long been touted as a health drink. The Egyptians used it to cure impotence, the Romans for constipation and as an aphrodisiac. Madame de Pompadour regularly fed Louis XV celery soup.

Peeling a celeriac root.

the spring and when night temperatures do not fall below 55°F.

If direct-seeding, make a small trench and fill with potting mix. Sprinkle seeds on top of the prepared soil and cover with ½ inch of soil. Keep moist until seedlings emerge, 10 to 20 days later.

Light
Full sun.

Soil
Humus-rich soil, kept moist during the growing season. Keep the soil pH at 6.0 to 6.5, a little acidic.

How to Grow
Fertilize celery monthly with applications of liquid fertilizer and keep up a consistent watering schedule. Keep beds well-weeded, but be careful not to disturb celery's shallow roots. Thin seedlings to 12 inches apart. Celeriac needs less water once it has become established and is growing well. As celery plants grow up to 10 to 12 inches, pile soil up 6 inches to blanch the stalks, making them sweeter and more tender.

If you want to blanch the lower stems, cover them with loose soil. You can also use cardboard or milk cartons.

Propagation
By seed. Or transplant young seedlings.

Pests and Diseases
Crop rotation prevents most problems. Watch for aphids and spray off with a jet of water.

Harvest
Celery matures in 80 to 100 days, and celeriac needs about 100 days to grow to harvest size. Harvest celery by cutting off outer stalks. In mild-winter gardens, do not harvest the head, but leave in garden, using just as needed. In spring, when the plants begin to bolt, harvest tender flower stalks

Homegrown celery has a taste and texture that's better than the store-bought product.

before they bloom. Harvest celeriac for storage when roots are 2 to 4 inches in width.

Storage
Store celery and celeriac in plastic in your refrigerator's crisper.

In the Kitchen
Use celery as a fresh crunchy vegetable or as a seasoning in soups and stews. As a vegetable, both celery and celeriac can be cooked until tender and served in a cream sauce. Cook celeriac and eat hot; it also adds a great "crunch" when cold in salads.

Other Uses
Dried celery leaves are strongly flavored; use them like celery seed as a seasoning. Save seeds and use as a spice.

Celeriac Salad

This is a typical first course in France.

2 celeriac bulbs
1 garlic clove
¼ cup mayonnaise

¼ teaspoon thyme
1 teaspoon lemon juice
Salt and pepper to taste

Peel the celeriac, cut into quarters and poach in boiling water until just tender, about 30 minutes. Add the garlic clove about halfway through and poach along with the celeriac. Drain and let cool. When cool enough to handle, discard the garlic and cut the celeriac into long, pencil-thick sticks.

In a small bowl, add the mayonnaise, thyme and lemon juice. If the dressing seems too thick, thin with water to the desired consistency. Mix well. Toss the celeriac with the dressing. Refrigerate for 2 hours or more to allow the flavors to develop. Salt and pepper to taste just before serving.

Serves 4.

COOKING GREENS:
COLLARDS, KALE, SWISS CHARD, SPINACH, NEW ZEALAND SPINACH

The flavor of collards and kale is improved by touches of frost. This is the hybrid collard 'Flash'.

Ten or 12 Swiss chard plants should supply a family of four. Make successive plantings every two or three weeks for young, tender plants.

We don't need the various institutes of health to inform us that many people don't eat enough greens. Greens don't sell at fast food joints, which is a shame. Greens are delicious. Plus, they supply us with potassium, calcium, vitamins A and C, iron and folic acid.

There is no reason to be without greens in your garden at any time.

Collards and kale are botanically the same plants. But collards, unlike kale, take summer heat without bolting. Collards and kale are very winter hardy, worth trying to grow from fall on, in all but the very coldest climates. In most gardens, collards and kale even stand up to a touch of snow.

Spinach is an early spring harvest, wilting with summer heat, while New Zealand spinach can be grown as a summer crop.

Swiss chard grows well almost year-round in mild-winter gardens, except in the hottest gardens.

Type
Grown as annuals, or in mild-winter climates as biennials.

Size
From 16 inches to 24 inches or larger depending upon variety.

Recommended Varieties
Just when there seems nothing new in the vegetable world along comes a new variety of unbeatable Swiss chard—(*Beta vulgaris*) 'Bright Lights'—with stems lit up in shades of yellow, pink and bright red. Extremely vigorous—it withstood eight days of hard frost in my garden—the

*True spinach (*Spinacia oleracea*) likes cool weather and rich, neutral soil. Make successive plantings every two weeks for a continual harvest. The hybrid 'Tyee' and the heirloom 'Bloomsdale Long Standing' are two favorite varieties.*

leaves are meaty but tender when quickly stir-fried.

Kale and collards are equally hardy, but unless harvested when the leaves are 3 to 4 inches long, the leaves become somewhat tough and need longer cooking.

A GIANT

Grown on the Channel Islands, the heirloom 'Giant Walking Stick' kale, *Brassica oleracea longata*, grows like a handsome bush 5 to 7 feet tall. Harvest the leaves along the stem or at the top. The stems, cut in the fall and then dried, produce a wood long used as walking sticks.

'Giant Walking Stick' kale before leaves are stripped off.

Simplest Greens Japanese-style

Simple flavors play up the rich taste of the greens in this dish, often served with spinach as the greens. It makes for a very special first course in some Japanese restaurants.

1 pound young, tender greens, mixed or all one type
3 tablespoons soy sauce
1 teaspoon white wine vinegar
3 tablespoons sesame seeds, toasted

Steam the greens for 3 to 5 minutes, or until they are cooked and fork tender. Toss them lightly with the soy sauce and vinegar. Let them cool. Serve them sprinkled with sesame seeds warm or at room temperature.

Serves 4 as a side dish.

'Winterbor' and 'Vates' are two kale varieties that winter well, although for tender leaves and rich flavor, the heirloom varieties, 'Red Russian' and 'Morris Heading' can't be beat. 'Champion' is a reliable and easily grown collard.

New Zealand spinach (*Tetragonia tetragonioides*) and Malabar spinach (*Basella alba*) are two vining plants that provide spinach-like greens during warm summer days, when regular spinach will long have gone to seed.

When to Plant
Early in spring or mid-summer for a fall harvest.

Light
Full sun in coastal climate areas, part shade in warm weather areas.

Soil
Humus-rich soil, kept moist during the growing season and with a pH of 6.5. Work in fertilizer before planting.

Kale is easy to grow in all but the hottest climates. It asks for little more than humus-rich soil and plenty of water (an inch a week).

How to Grow
Transplant seedlings or direct sow early in spring; thin according to type of plant. Sow again in mid-summer for a fall harvest. When transplanting, keep seedlings well watered.

Propagation
Seed or transplant seedlings.

Pests and Diseases
Enclose young plants with floating row covers to keep root maggots away. Spray with Bt when you see cabbage moths fluttering around plants.

Harvest
Cut off outer leaves at soil level to continue harvest.

Try brightly colored chard plants in the ornamental garden, or in containers.

Storage
Store in a cool dark place or the crisper of the refrigerator for no more than 1 to 2 days.

In the Kitchen
Use the small leaves of these greens fresh in salads. When leaves are larger, stir-fry or steam them. Simmer tougher, mature leaves with ham hocks to eat with beans or in soups or stews. "Hopping John" is a Southern dish of beans and greens eaten on New Year's day to bring good luck and good fortune for the rest of the year.

Kale is ornamental and nutritious, too, with three times the vitamin C of spinach.

CORN

Zea mays

Seven thousand years ago, savvy farmers in Mesoamerica began to cross-breed grasses to make a larger and larger seed pod. Columbus mentions corn in his journal after he met the Taino, the native inhabitants of the New World. They called their sustaining grain *mahiz*, and throughout most of the world it is still called maize. The Aztecs, Mayans and Incas perfected cultivation and preservation techniques, continually cross-breeding to improve the harvest. Through time, corn has spread throughout the Americas in many different shapes and colors.

Corn was a sacred food to a number of tribes of Native Americans. Many ceremonies and sacred dances, such as the corn dance of the New Mexico Pueblos, celebrate corn's life-giving importance. The Iroquois planted corn on hills, letting it grow about half a foot before they then started seeds of squash and beans, which used the tall corn as poles to climb up. The Zuni still grow a blue kernel corn. When ground and mixed into a gruel thinly spread on a griddle, it produces a thin flat bread called *piki*.

Also popular in ancient times was popcorn, and today's 'Baby Blue' and 'Calico' both make delicious snacks.

The average American eats about 30 pounds of corn annually. Figure on 1 1/2 to two ears per plant when you plan your garden.

Type
Annual.

Size
From 4-foot popcorn varieties to 8- or 10-feet-tall heirloom varieties.

Recommended Varieties
Hybridizers have developed ultra-sweet flavored varieties of corn collectively known as the "supersweets." Supersweets initially won gardeners over with their sugar-sweet flavor which lasts longer than other varieties due to its delay in conversion of sugar to starch. But supersweets were finicky in their cultivation requirements, and had to be isolated from other corn types to keep from cross-pollinating.

'Silver Queen' is a popular midseason (90 days to maturity) corn cultivar with whitish kernels.

'Mohawk Blue' is a beautiful ornamental corn.

'Hopi Blue' and 'Renewal' are heirloom flour corns, with easy-to-grind soft kernels.

Personally, I prefer the old-fashioned corn types like 'Silver Queen', or 'Early Sunglow'. Plant different varieties in your garden for a succession of corn all through the summer. Try other varieties if you have room. Look for broom straw, podded corn or heirloom types like 'Bloody Butcher', 'Baby Blue' or 'Black Amber'.

When to Plant

When the soil warms in the spring and when night temperatures do not fall below 50°F.

As you might guess from its name, 'Sweetie' is a supersweet hybrid.

Soil temperature should be 65°F. Wait until the soil is 70°F to plant super-sweet corn. If you prefer, start seeds indoors four to six weeks before soil is ready for planting.

Light

Full sun.

Soil

Humus-rich soil, kept moist during the growing season. Enrich soil with fertilizer before planting and mulch with 4 to 6 inches of organic compost when plants are 12 inches tall.

'Kandy Korn' is a "sugary enhanced" hybrid—it can be grown without isolation from other corn varieties.

'Bloody Butcher' is an heirloom that's best used to grind into flour or as roasting ears.

You'll know the ears of corn are ripening when the silk browns.

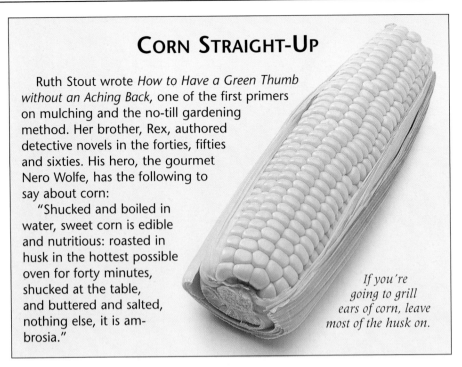

CORN STRAIGHT-UP

Ruth Stout wrote *How to Have a Green Thumb without an Aching Back*, one of the first primers on mulching and the no-till gardening method. Her brother, Rex, authored detective novels in the forties, fifties and sixties. His hero, the gourmet Nero Wolfe, has the following to say about corn:

"Shucked and boiled in water, sweet corn is edible and nutritious: roasted in husk in the hottest possible oven for forty minutes, shucked at the table, and buttered and salted, nothing else, it is ambrosia."

If you're going to grill ears of corn, leave most of the husk on.

How to Grow

Plant corn in short rows, making blocks of at least 4 rows to assure pollination. Soak the seeds overnight. In well prepared soil, draw your finger in a line through the moist soil to create a trough 1½ inches deep. Sow the seeds 1 to 2 inches deep in the trough, spacing them 4 inches apart. Rows should be 30 inches apart. Cover the trough with soil and pat down firmly. After the seeds are 6 inches high, thin them to every 8 inches. When growing tall corn, mound up soil around roots after they grow to 12 inches to encourage further root development.

Fertilize the corn when it is 6 to 8 inches high, using a high-nitrogen soluble organic fertilizer according to the container's directions. Water regularly and increase watering when the tassels emerge from

the stalk, to ensure growth of the kernels.

Propagation

By seed or transplant seedlings.

Pests and Diseases

Netting may be necessary to keep birds from eating seedlings.

Raccoons can destroy a corn crop with night raids just as the corn is ripening. Electric fencing may deter them.

Most hybrid corn resists disease. Although corn borers are a pest, their damage is usually minimal. Simply cut off the end of the corn where they have been.

What could be more inviting than a steaming, buttery hunk of cornbread made from homegrown corn?

Ornamental corns are also known as Indian corn. Most stay on the stalk until they're dry, and thus need a longer season—usually more than 110 days.

TIP

ONLY FRESH WILL DO

Here are old-time instructions for cooking corn. First start the water boiling. Once the water boils, pick the corn. Run all the way back to the kitchen as you peel the corn. If you trip, throw the corn away and start all over again. The moral: Sweet corn is at its absolute best when fresh picked!

Harvest corn as close as possible to when you'll be cooking it. It can't be too fresh!

Harvest

About three weeks after the first silk appears, when milky juice squirts out of a kernel. The silk will start to brown and dry.

Storage

Cook corn immediately. To dry it for future use, pull back the husks, strip off the silk and hang the ears in long chains out of the direct sun in a warm dry place.

In the Kitchen

Eating fresh raw corn, as a salad, will convince you that you don't always need to cook it. Grill corn on the cob, pickle the cut-off kernels, or scrape off the corn and cook as a pudding.

Other Uses

In Central America, corn stars in ice cream, which seems strange for the first few bites but then becomes positively addictive. Baking with corn in fritters, cornbread and pancakes adds another dimension to its culinary persona. Try scorching the corn for a rich, caramelized flavor before adding it to your recipes. Simply stir the corn in a skillet over medium heat until it begins to turn golden brown. If the corn begins to stick to the pan, add a small amount of oil.

Red Pepper and Corn Relish

This relish uses the sweet/hot/sour flavoring base of Asian pickles, but adds the down-home ingredients corn and red peppers.

4 cups corn, freshly cut off the cob
½ cup diced sweet red peppers
4 red chile peppers, slit lengthwise
4 bay leaves
4 garlic cloves
2½ cups 5-percent vinegar

1 cup water
1 cup sugar
2 tablespoons salt
1 tablespoon coarsely ground black pepper

Mix the corn and the peppers together. Divide the corn-pepper mixture evenly between 4 pint jars. Add a chile pepper, bay leaf and garlic clove to each jar.

To a medium sized saucepan, add vinegar, water, sugar, salt and pepper. Bring this brine mixture to a boil. Pour the hot brine to the jars of corn, leaving about ½ inch head space. Wipe the rim of the jars clean and screw on the lid and band. Process the corn in a steam canner or a hot water bath for 15 minutes. Remove the jars and place on a clean towel to cool. After the jars have cooled, check the lids to make sure they have sealed properly.

Store for at least one month in a cool, dark place before opening.

Makes 4 pints.

CUCUMBERS

Cucumis sativus

Cucumbers need lots of sun and a rich soil full of humus.

It is hard to imagine that the cucumber would have a wildly controversial history. Although loved by the Romans, cucumbers almost disappeared from cultivation along with the Roman empire.

The famous diarist, Samuel Pepys, suggests various deaths from overeating of cucumbers, "cowcumbers," and the coolness with which they are always linked was blamed for bringing on ague and even impotence.

Henry V's Spanish wife, Catherine of Aragon, introduced cucumbers to England. And Columbus planted cucumbers in the new world, where they took hold and flourished. Another cucumber enthusiast, Henry J. Heinz, began commercially pickling cucumbers in the late 19th Century. The pickle became ubiq-uitous. Any collector of Victorian sterling silver can boast of pickling forks, specially shaped forks with three prongs to stab pickles and deliver them to a plate.

Cucumbers themselves have almost no nutritional value, as they are mostly water. If they are not grown well or kept too long, they can develop a bitter tang reminiscent of their ancient cucumber ancestors from the Himalayan Mountains.

Type
Annual.

Size
Vines can be 4 feet long and just as wide, perfect for trellising. Bush types grow just 2 feet long.

Recommended Varieties
Plant a variety of cucumbers from slicing cucumbers to the tiny cornichons (tiny cucumbers). Try the cornichon 'Vert de Massy' or larger pickling gherkins such as 'Saladin'. Try 'Salad Bush' for a compact vine. Grow the burpless types such as 'Tasty Green' or 'Amira', a very prolific, disease-resistant variety.

Although the 3- to 4-inch, bright-yellow globes of the lemon cucumbers are attractive, their taste isn't as good as other varieties. 'Painted Serpent' cucumber, a rediscovered heirloom variety, is the antithesis of the hybridizers' goal to develop the straightest cucumber possible.

When to Plant
When the soil warms in the spring and when night temperatures do not fall below 50°F.

Light
Full sun.

Soil
Rich, well-drained soil with plenty of well-rotted compost worked in at least 2 weeks before planting. Cucumbers are very

Pick cucumbers young for the freshest, tenderest flavor.

Hot Summer, Cold Cucumber Mint Soup

4 large cucumbers, peeled, halved and seeded
3 garlic cloves, peeled
2 cups chicken broth, homemade or canned
1 pint yogurt
2 teaspoons finely chopped mint
Salt and freshly ground pepper to taste

Cut the cucumbers into equal-sized chunks. Add the cucumbers, chicken broth and garlic to a medium-size saucepan. Simmer the cucumbers and garlic, covered, over low heat for 20 minutes or until the cucumbers are tender when pierced with a fork. Remove the pan from the heat and let cool. In a blender or food processor, add the cucumbers, garlic and broth. Blend for 2 minutes. Add the yogurt and the mint, and blend again for 30 seconds. If the soup seems too thick, add a bit more broth or yogurt. Salt and pepper to taste. Serve chilled.

Serves 4.

heavy feeders: side dress every two weeks with liquid fertilizer.

How to Grow

For hill planting, mound the soil in the prepared planting area to form a round bed that is 2 feet in diameter and about 6 inches higher than the normal soil level. Sow four seeds on each hill, pushing them down 1 inch deep. Pat the soil down firmly. Thin to the 2 strongest seedlings when plants are 3 inches high. Leave 5 feet between hills. Cucumbers do well trained on trellises or netting, which supports the growing cucumbers.

Propagation

By seed or transplants. The *Cucumis* family cross-pollinates, so any seed-saving must be done

carefully. Hand-pollinate flowers and then tie up blooms to prevent any additional pollination from wind or insects.

Pests and Diseases

Watch out for the striped cucumber beetle, and hand pick. Cucumbers are susceptible to mildew, but most of the hybrids are resistant. Choose varieties carefully if mildew is a problem in your garden.

Harvest

From 50 to 80 days, depending upon variety. Pick cornichons at 3 inches, gherkins at 4 to 6 inches long, and long types at 12 to 15 inches. Continued picking extends the harvest.

Storage

Cucumbers do not store well. For the freshest, sweetest taste,

Kids can grow cucumbers fairly easily. When growing them in a container, choose bush varieties and provide support.

Give cucumbers plenty of water when they're flowering—at least one inch a week.

They're often still regarded as a novelty, but 'Lemon' cucumbers have been around long enough to qualify as an heirloom.

use within one to two days of picking.

In the Kitchen

From pickles to quick sautées to salads, cucumbers have a permanent place in the kitchen. If you miss a cucumber and it grows too large, poach and purée it for cold soup.

Other Uses

Cucumbers make great salsas with a sweet/hot flavoring of vinegar, sugar and hot chiles.

EDIBLE FLOWERS

Flowers in your cooking add a dash of fantasy and a pinch of whimsy. Edible flowers are not a new idea, just a recycled one. They contribute flavor, texture and color to cooked and fresh dishes, tisanes and sugar syrups.

The Earl of Devonshire served up peonies to his guests at his wedding breakfast in 1389. Cooks in the Middle Ages depended upon flowers for their salads. When Cortez first reached Tenochtitlan, now Mexico City, he was served dishes prepared with exotic ingredients such as chocolate, chiles and flowers. Chinese cooks today still stir-fry dried daylily buds.

We mention just a few easily-grown, edible flowers here. But be warned: Not all flowers are edible, and some flowers and their leaves can be deadly poisonous, as lethal as choosing the wrong type of mushroom. Use only flowers known to be edible!

Variety of Harvest

Borage (*Borago officinalis*)
The blue, star-shaped flowers of the annual borage were often pictured in medieval illuminated manuscripts. Pluck the flowers off the hairy stem and scatter them on the top of soups or in salads. For a cooling summer iced tea, freeze bright

Rose petals have been used in the kitchen for thousands of years.

blue blossoms in lemonade ice cubes.

Calendula (*Calendula officinalis*)
The bright daisy-like flowers come in colors from butter yellow to pumpkin orange. Use the petals raw or dried.

Johnny Jump-Up (*Viola tricolor*)
A charming tiny, monkey-faced plant. The blossoms come in a range of blues, purples, and bicolors. Once established, Johnny jump-ups re-seed themselves. Use them to edge beds, or let them romp wild through the vegetable garden. Strew the tiny blossoms over salads, place on top of iced cakes or scatter over dessert plates.

Rose (*Rosa* spp.)
Fragrant rose petals can be candied, cooked with sugar for syrup, or left in sugar to perfume it subtly. Use rose petals fresh or dried, but first cut out the bitter white triangle at each petal's base. Grind dried petals and mix with powdered sugar to sprinkle over cookies and cakes.

Type
Annuals, with the exception of roses, which are perennials.

Size
From 6 inches to the spreading height of the rose shrubs or climbing vines, depending upon variety.

Johnny jump-ups like average soil and will take part shade.

Nasturtiums are colorful and edible flowers, and the leaves are a bonus— both taste like watercress. Watch for bugs inside the blooms!

Recommended Varieties

Like mushrooms, eat only flowers experts list as edible.

When to Plant

Early spring.

Light

At least 4 to 6 hours of sun a day.

Borage has beautiful purple flowers that would grace an ornamental bed. The flowers of most culinary herbs make versatile kitchen companions.

Soil

Humus-rich soil, kept moist during the growing season.

How to Grow

Plant seeds or transplants in early spring and water consistently.

Roses, however, need more careful treatment. Pull leaves from stems in the middle of the plant to increase air circulation; this will decrease the chance of disease. Fertilize monthly and keep well weeded. Prune in late winter.

Propagation

Seed or transplant seedlings, except for the rose. Plant a bareroot rose in earliest spring, container roses through the growing season.

Pests and Diseases

Few diseases affect the annuals. Mildew, black spot or rust may affect roses. Wash off aphids with a strong jet of water.

Harvest

Harvest flowers in the morning just after the dew has dried. Cut when flowers are just starting to bloom, the period when the essential oils are at their peak. Dry the cut blooms upside down in a brown paper sack in a warm, dark area, or use a dehydrator.

Storage

Use fresh flowers the day they are picked. Store dried flowers in a cool, dark place inside a sealed glass container. For the strongest fragrance, try not to crumble petals. Discard after 6 months.

Relatives of Johnny jump-ups and violets, violas are edible too.

In the Kitchen

Use flowers raw or dried in cooked dishes, in salads, as decorations for dessert plates or float them in iced drinks. Calendula petals can be added to scrambled eggs or cooked with rice, or float the whole flower in lemonade. Sprinkle petals of calendula on top of an icy-cold vichyssoise or cucumber soup, add them to baked breads or work them into butter for confetti bursts of color.

Scatter Johnny jump-ups around a fresh lettuce salad or arrange them around the top of a cake for a dainty touch.

Other Uses

Plant these flowers in the flower border, or interplant among the vegetables to add splashes of color. All the flowers grow successfully in containers.

A bowl of May wine with Johnny jump-ups.

Flowered Ice Cubes

Fill an ice cube tray with water or lemonade. Sprinkle in a variety of flowers. Freeze for use in water glasses or iced tea. Mint tea, with its ethereal pale green color, shows off these ice cubes beautifully.

EGGPLANTS

Solanum melongena

Eggplants are native to south central Asia, probably India. Seeing the big, purple fruits makes the name "eggplant" peculiar unless you know that the name came from an ancestor which was white and, of course, egg-shaped.

The culinary journey from India to Europe was slow. Since eggplant was long thought to induce madness, they were typically ignored. In 1753, Linnaeus (who set up the original classification system for plant, and animal life) first called eggplant *Solanum insanum*. He then changed it to *Solanum melongena*, which means "soothing mad apple," for reasons not understood. Finally, by the 19th century, the eggplant had its own section in all the early cookbooks, primarily featured as a breakfast dish.

Today's eggplants come in all sizes, shapes and colors. Find the warmest part of the garden for them. If your climate is on the cool side, plant the new, tiny eggplants that produce well in cooler temperatures. Cover them with a row cloth to boost temperatures and consequently yield. Try eggplants with white and pink stripes, the long purples, or the all white or pure orange.

Type
Perennial, grown as annual.

Eggplants come in a world of colors and shapes. Try several kinds in your ornamental/edible garden.

Size
From 2½-foot bush-types excellent for containers to larger 3-foot bushes.

Recommended Varieties
The new baby "finger" eggplants are easy to grow, and delicious grilled. Look for 'Little Fingers', or the longer Asian types such as' Machiaw' or 'Asian Bride'. 'Rosa Bianca' is one of the loveliest eggplant varieties; it has a delicate pink blush and a fine flavor.

When to Plant
When the soil warms in the spring and night temperatures do not fall below 50°F.

Light
Full sun.

Soil
Humus-rich soil, kept moist during the growing season. Eggplants need nitrogen enriched

Pick the fruits of eggplant when they're small and have a glossy sheen.

Many cooks salt down freshly cut eggplant slices, especially of the larger fruits, to draw out bitterness. Rinse off and pat the slices dry before you cook them.

Simple Grilled Eggplant

4 Japanese eggplants, unpeeled
4 teaspoons Asian sesame oil
2 teaspoons toasted sesame seeds

Grill the eggplants over a medium heat until they feel soft and well-cooked, about 5 to 7 minutes. Remove from the fire and make a thin cut in each eggplant from top to bottom. Add a teaspoon of sesame oil inside each cut. Sprinkle the sesame seeds over the tops and serve immediately.

Asian or Japanese eggplants generally have thinner skins that you don't have to peel.

'Rosa Bianca' is an Italian heirloom that cooks love to use: It's reportedly free of bitterness.

soil, so work in high-nitrogen fertilizer before planting.

How to Grow

Use black plastic mulch or row covers to increase soil temperatures for excellent growth and to assure good fruit set. Space plants about 24 inches apart; rows should be at least 24 inches apart.

Propagation

Seed or transplant seedlings. Seeds need soil temperatures of 80°F to germinate; use a heating mat underneath seedling trays for best results.

Pests and Diseases

Eggplants are very hardy and also disease- and pest-resistant. Enclose young plants with floating row covers to keep insects and flea beetles away, as well as to boost temperatures.

Harvest

Pick eggplants when they stop swelling and develop a glossy sheen. To continue harvest, pick eggplants when they are small.

Storage

Use as soon as possible; overripe eggplants are bitter.

In the Kitchen

Eggplants are wonderfully versatile. They taste fine grilled, stuffed, baked or puréed. Because of its long culinary journey, you will find recipes for eggplant in cuisines around the world.

TIP GRILL IT, BROIL IT

When fried, eggplant can sop up oil in outrageous amounts. Try grilling eggplant instead of frying it. Here's how:

Cut the eggplant into ½-inch thick slices and brush a light touch of olive oil across the surface. Grill both sides until the slices are tender. You can also broil eggplant the same way; turn after the first side browns, to cook both sides.

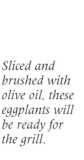

Sliced and brushed with olive oil, these eggplants will be ready for the grill.

FENNEL:
FLORENCE FENNEL OR FINOCCHIO
Foeniculum vulgare

This is the bulb fennel, eaten for the crisp, delicious and fleshy base. The over-lapping leaves form a bulb above the ground known as the apple, which also describes the crisp, crunchy texture. Although Italian cooks have always loved using fennel, it has taken some time to catch on in America.

The whole plant is edible. The bulb can be thinly sliced for salad or braised for a buttery, rich hot dish. The stalks with their stronger flavor can be used like celery to flavor long-simmering dishes, while the ferny tops can season like dill. If you let the plants go to seed, the spicy, anise-tasting seeds are delicious.

Type
Perennial, grown as annual.

Size
12 to 18 inches high.

Recommended Varieties
Try the heirloom 'Romy' or 'Zefa Fino'.

When to Plant
Sow seeds directly in the ground in early spring, or plant mid-summer for a fall crop.

Light
Full sun.

Florence fennel's graceful form makes it welcome in both the vegetable bed and the ornamental garden.

Bulb fennel is a good choice for containers or raised beds. It also attracts swallowtail butterflies.

Florence fennel bulbs slice into delicious, anise-flavored rings. These slices can be used fresh or cooked.

Soil

Humus-rich soil, kept moist during the growing season.

How to Grow

Sow plants ½ inch deep, where they are to grow. Thin to 6 inches apart after seedlings sprout. Water regularly. Clip off any flower stalks that appear.

Propagation

Seed or transplant seedlings grown in individual cellpacks. Fennel doesn't like to have its roots disturbed.

Pests and Diseases

Will attract larvae of the swallowtail butterfly.

Harvest

Wait for bulbs to become fist-sized to harvest, about 80 days. Cut off any seed stalks. Cut at soil level or pull out the whole plant.

Storage

Store for one week in the crisper drawer of the refrigerator.

In the Kitchen

Use thin slices for salads, bake along side roasts or braise for fine flavors.

Harvest the entire plant. Cut off the greens and use them in salads or as a wrap or garnish for fish dishes.

Fennel and Orange Salad

This makes a winter salad that pairs well with rich stews and soups. Blood oranges provide intense flavor, but if they are not available, use sweet navel oranges. Winter onions can be overly strong; soaking the onion slices in cold water takes away the harsh flavor.

1 fennel bulb, about ½ pound
1 small red onion, about ¼ pound
2 large blood or navel oranges
3 tablespoons fragrant olive oil
1 teaspoon red wine vinegar
¼ teaspoon salt
Freshly ground pepper to taste

Trim off the bottom and top of the fennel bulb and slice as thin as possible across the bulb. Discard any tough centers.

Peel and thinly slice the onion in rings. If the onion has a very strong flavor, soak the rings in cold water for 15 minutes to sweeten them. With a knife, cut off the peel of the oranges, making sure to trim off any white pith remaining. Slice the oranges across in ¼-inch-thick pieces. Place the fennel, onion rings and orange slices in a salad bowl. Add the olive oil and toss gently to mix well. Add the red wine vinegar, the salt and pepper and toss again. Serve immediately or refrigerate for up to four hours before using.

Serves 4.

GARLIC

Allium sativum

What is beloved by chefs and vampire hunters? What was on the pyramid at Cheops? What was fed to Roman soldiers as a part of their daily rations? Garlic, of course!

Touted as a cure against witches and vampires, garlic was braided and hung on doors to ward off evil spirits during medieval times. Recipes for cooking garlic were found on Mesopotamian tablets dating from 1700 B.C. Garlic is now under scientific study as a medicinal cure to various physical problems from the common cold to lowering high blood pressure and cholesterol.

Type
Bulb, grown as annual.

Size
Up to 2 feet.

Recommended Varieties
'Sicilian' garlic is a white-skinned, soft-necked variety, resistant to bolting. One 'Sicilian' garlic bulb produces a large har-

'Italian' garlic is a vigorous performer that stores well.

vest of cloves that whirl around the central stem. 'Italian', another soft neck, is a long-keeping variety with large, hard-to-peel, plump cloves.

For stiff-neck types, look for the chefs' favorite red type such as 'Spanish Roja' with its excellent flavor and easy-to-peel cloves. However, it does not keep as long as white varieties. 'German Red' likes a colder climate than the 'Spanish Roja' and is also very easy to peel, with fair storing properties. 'Creole Red' has great flavor, peels easily and matures early in the season.

When to Plant
Plant in autumn.

Light
Full sun.

Soil
Work in plenty of organic compost just before planting so your soil drains well but retains moisture. Garlic likes moist, humus-rich soil with a pH of about 6.5.

How to Grow
A fall planting of garlic will bring you a harvest the following summer. Plant the separated cloves before the ground gets too wet and too cold for the garlic to become established. Plant the pointed end of the clove up, and set the cloves 2 inches deep and 4 inches apart. Add a slow-release, pelleted, organic fertilizer high in potassium and phosphorus. Mulch the bed to protect the cloves if you live in a cold climate.

Propagation
Although you can plant organic garlic from grocery markets, it is best to use garlic ready for planting from nurseries or

A clove a day keeps all kinds of maladies away, say researchers. For flavor, homegrown garlic beats store-bought, hands down.

specialty catalogs. Garlic starts are quite expensive, so it is always a good idea to save some of your harvest for the next planting year. Divide whole garlic bulbs and choose the plumpest, largest cloves to plant.

Pests and Diseases
Garlic is relatively pest- and disease-free.

Harvest
Harvest your garlic in the late spring to early summer. When you notice the stems of the garlic starting to brown, stop watering. When the tops fall over, start to carefully dig the bulbs out of the garden. Tie the stems together in loose clumps and keep them in the shade until the bulbs harden and the stalks dry. Sort out any damaged bulbs for immediate use. Braid up the soft-necked varieties. Cut the stalks off the stiff-necked

For braiding, harvest your bulbs before the leaves get tough and fibrous. Cure bulbs in a darkish, dry, airy and warm location for a couple of weeks.

TIP

ELEPHANT GARLIC

Elephant Garlic (*Allium ampeloprasum*) is technically a member of the onion family. But because of its flavor and growing habit, this bulb is called a garlic. It produces immense cloves, as its name poetically declares. Some bulbs grow to 1½ pounds! Hard-core garlic aficionados don't like the flavor, finding it too bland.

Elephant garlic is a larger, but milder, relative of true garlic.

Baked Garlic

Baked garlic becomes a kind of spread—almost buttery—in consistency. You can squeeze out cloves on top of crackers or baked toasts. Or use it instead of butter on baked potatoes. Stir with cream and add as a swirled topping to hot soups. Squeeze out cloves on warm French bread for a divine treat. There is no end of uses.

4 whole heads of garlic
1 tablespoon olive oil
Salt and pepper

Preheat the oven to 350°F.
Peel off the outer layers of papery skin. Cut off the top ½ inch of the garlic. Brush the surfaces with olive oil. Salt and pepper the heads. Place the heads on a cookie sheet and bake for 45 minutes to 1 hour, or until the garlic is a golden brown. Break off a clove and squeeze out the baked garlic. Serve with crackers, toast, or use as a topping!

Serves 4.

varieties just above the garlic head.

Storage

Store garlic in a cool, dark, well-ventilated area. Red varieties will keep about four months, white varieties for ten to twelve months.

Care

Water regularly to bring your garlic to a robust harvest. If you are growing the stiff-necked garlic varieties, your garlic will send up a flowering stalk in the late spring. This twists and turns at first, then stands up straight and stiffens. For maximum bulb size, cut off the stalk before it stiffens.

USES FOR FRESH GARLIC

1. Drop three or four cloves in vinegar for a garlic-infused flavor in salad dressings.

2. Separate cloves and blanch garlic in boiling water for 3 to 4 minutes. Pop the cloves out of their skins and stuff them into pickled peppers or pitted olives and restore them to their brine.

Use the stuffed peppers or olives as spicy additions to martinis or antipasto plates.

3. Keep a jar of poached garlic in the refrigerator. Use the poached garlic in salad dressings, pesto or salsas to avoid the bitter taste of raw cloves.

In the Kitchen

There are recipes for using garlic in everything from garlic soup to garlic ice cream. Try poaching garlic briefly before using, for a smoother flavor; this makes it easier to peel as well. Poach several heads at a time and store them in a covered container in the refrigerator.

Other Uses

Many people eat not only the bulb, but also the leaves of garlic (known as green garlic). So your planting can reap two harvests!

Each of these garlic bulbs was grown from a single clove—about a ten-fold return.

You can harvest some of the leaves from your garlic plants. Use them as you would chives, but remember that their flavor is more zesty.

'Spanish Roja' produces plump, full-of-flavor cloves.

CULINARY HERBS

Herb gardens can be formal or informal, as long as it's sunny. Compared with most plants, herbs don't really need rich soil or a lot of help to flourish.

Fresh bay leaves are a world apart from the dried ones in jars. Try growing this evergreen as a container plant if your climate is colder than Zone 8.

What would our food taste like without herbs? Who was the first chef to pluck off a strong smelling leaf and drop it into a pot simmering over the fire?

Herbs have accompanied our food from time immemorial. And since they grow like sturdy weeds, herbs make wonderful garden residents.

You can squeeze herbs in just about anywhere in the garden. Herbs don't mind poor soil, and many varieties are drought resistant. In fact, given a bit of water, the herbs in the mint family become invasive. No amount of harvesting for mint teas and jelly keeps them under control! They, like other herbs, also grow contentedly in containers, an excellent way to keep a supply without having your garden overrun.

Whether you choose to plant your herbs in the ground or in containers, place them near the kitchen or back door for easy access. Fresh herbs, direct from the garden to the pot, are unmatched in flavor.

An Herb Hall of Fame

Basil and Scented Basils (*Ocimum basilicum*)

Basil is the main ingredient in pesto. Less well-known basils such as cinnamon and anise add flavor to every course, from soup to a basil-infused sugar syrup for fruits. Basil prefers rich soil and regular watering. Purple basil has a more cinnamon flavor and dark purple leaves, which color vinegar a glorious sunset pink.

Fresh basil belongs in the kitchen any time. Try overwintering a few plants for kitchen use, or start seeds for new plants on the windowsill.

Bay (*Laurus nobilis*)

An easily grown evergreen shrub or small tree with fragrant leaves and classic flavor. Bay trees cannot stand harsh, snowy winters but since they adapt well to container culture, no household needs to be without one. Simply overwinter the container indoors in a bright, light area. The fresh leaves have a sweet taste, much better than the dried ones purchased from stores.

'Opal' basil is a colorful plant in vegetable, ornamental or herb beds, or grown as a specimen in containers.

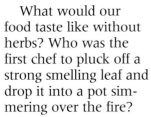

Bergamot (*Monarda didyma*)

A native American species also known as bee balm or Oswego tea. Grow it for the fragrant leaves and splashy flowers. This plant needs a moist soil and will take part shade. Brew alone for a tea fragrant with the essence of flowers, or add leaves to black tea for an herbal Earl Gray tea.

Chamomile (*Chamaemelum nobile*)

The English variety is a perennial, growing to 1 foot. The German variety is an annual. Use the blossoms for tisanes.

Chamomile makes a beautiful ground-cover and a soothing tea—just ask Peter Rabbit.

Coriander, also known as Cilantro (*Coriandrum sativum*)

An easily grown herb used in Mexican cooking, salsas and Asian cuisine. Look for 'Slo-bolt' and grow in the cooler seasons or in part shade in warmer times of the year. If the plants bolt, let them go to seed: delicious seasoning in its own right. Sow every two weeks for successive harvests.

Cilantro, also called coriander or Chinese parsley, will give you a continous supply of pungent leaves if you make successive plantings.

Lavender's unique scent and flavor have made it a welcome member of the edible garden.

Lavender (*Lavandula* spp.)

The name lavender comes from the Roman word lavo, which means "to wash." The ancient Greeks and Romans used the herb to scent their baths. Lavender was also used in the great halls of medieval fiefdoms in the days before the luxury of indoor plumbing.

Lavender grows well in containers. Water consistently. Fertilize and prune after the plant blooms. If you wish to use the blossoms, cut the bloom stalks in the morning just as the dew has dried, and hang them upside down in a warm, dark place to dry.

There are English, French and Spanish varieties of lavender, but the English is generally considered to be the most fragrant. Lavender has been enjoying a revival as a culinary herb. Add the flowers to butter cookies, throw stalks onto the grill for an aromatic smoke, or add bloom heads to marinades and salad vinegars.

Lemon grass is a tender native of the Indian subcontinent, so if you live in Zone 8 or colder, try it in containers and bring it in for the winter.

Lemon Grass (*Cymbopogon citratus*)

Long used in Asian cuisine, lemon grass grows into a handsome landscape plant with 2- to 3-foot-long leaves. Lemon grass is tender, so grow it in a container and winter it in a protected spot.

Lemon Verbena (*Aloysia triphylla*)

A partly deciduous, large perennial shrub that grows to 4 feet. Likes full sun and some water all summer long. Can be grown in the ground or in containers. Harvest by pinching back the leaf tips. Imparts intense lemony flavor fresh or dried to teas or marinades. It is tender, so grow in containers where winters are harsh, and move indoors to protect it against the cold.

Lemon verbena is pretty, full of flavor, and tender. It's hardy in Zones 9 to 11 but can be a container plant or annual in colder regions.

Mints come in more and more flavors every year. This is apple mint, a great ingredient in iced tea.

Mints (*Mentha* spp.)

Spearmint, peppermint, orange mint, even chocolate mints are available. These are invasive perennials, so plant carefully in restricted beds or use in containers. Variegated mints are also available. All like some water and will take shade.

Parsley, Italian or Curly (*Petroselinum crispum*)

Most know the curly parsley that garnishes plates, but there is also the stronger-flavored Italian or flat-leaf parsley. Parsley is well worth eating, since it is full of iron and vitamins A, C and E. Besides its culinary uses, curled parsley can edge beds or line parterres. Italian parsley grows tall. Both types provide flowers when they bolt, attracting beneficial insects. Parsley is slow to germinate—up to 21 days—so continue to water sown seeds to give them time to sprout.

Rosemary (*Rosmarinus offficinalis*)

This tender perennial, hardy to 10°F, can be a tall hedge or a draping groundcover. Useful as a landscape tool, or as a fine container plant, rosemary shines in the kitchen with strong resinous flavors. Rosemary branches can perfume meats or vegetables

Rosemary sprigs make wonderful flavorings for grilled items or for flavored oils and vinegars.

when tossed on top of charcoal just before adding items to grill. Added to vinegars, rosemary lends a special fragrance to salads. Roasted vegetables with rosemary are memorable.

Rosemary in its creeping form makes a beautiful hedge or massed planting.

"Why should a man die when he has a plant of sage?" goes one ancient saying.

Sage (*Salvia* spp.)

A perennial shrub which may die back in cooler winters. Wants dry soil. Look for the purple, pink, green and white variegated varieties to add color to the garden. Pinch the leaves back to shape.

Italian or flat-leaf parsley has lots more flavor than curly types.

GROW A ROSEMARY TOPIARY INSIDE

Rosemary is best known as the herb of remembrance. Throughout the Middle Ages, brides gave it to their bridegrooms as a token of fidelity, and rosemary was added to bridal cakes. Warm sprigs of rosemary in the oven or simmer them with juniper berries on a warm radiator in winter if you want a lively and instant room fragrance that doesn't come out of a bottle. Sprigs dropped into a steamy bath stimulate and refresh both body and spirit.

Prune your rosemary plant in any shape you wish. Triangles or ball shapes are fun. Place your rosemary topiary in a sunny window. Prune regularly to help keep its shape, using the clipped leaves in cooking or bathing.

Place the container where it receives four hours of sun a day and keep the soil moist but not soggy. Fertilize every two weeks with a soluble organic fertilizer diluted to half strength. If you have a suitable location, let the plant summer outside.

Lemon thyme is just one of the many flavored thymes. There are several different forms too.

Thyme (*Thymus vulgaris*)

The primary culinary herb variety. This 8- to 12-inch-high perennial with small blue-gray leaves can be used to edge beds. It trims into neat mounds and never becomes invasive.

Type

Most herbs are perennials, but some varieties are not hardy and are treated as annuals.

Size

From ground hugging up to 4 feet tall, depending upon variety.

Recommended Varieties

Innumerable varieties.

When to Plant

Spring in cold-weather areas, fall in mild-winter locations.

Light

From part shade to full sun depending upon variety.

Soil

Humus-rich soil, but most herbs are not fussy.

How to Grow

Most herbs grow almost like weeds. Do not over fertilize. Prune herbs back after they flower.

Propagation

By seed, root cuttings or stem prunings.

Pests and Diseases

Most herbs are rarely disturbed by pests.

Harvest

Harvest herbs in the morning after the dew has dried. Cut when flowers are just starting to bloom, the period when the essential oils are at their peak. Dry the cut blooms by hanging upside down in a warm, dark area. Leaves, when harvested, can be dried in a dehydrator or in a microwave oven. (See page 136).

Storage

Store in a cool dark place inside a sealed glass container. For the strongest fragrance, try not to crumble leaves or flowers. Discard after 6 months.

In the Kitchen

Use in teas, infusions, marinades and of course, as seasoning on everything.

Other Uses

Herbs are used to discourage moths, as medicinal agents and as relaxants or sleep enhancers. In fact, herbs star in many different products, and are under renewed scientific scrutiny to discover the full extent of their usefulness to humankind.

Herb Salt

John Ash, a noted Northern California chef and cookbook author, created this blend as an herb rub for roasted poultry. But with a bit of adjustment (incorporated below), it makes a delicious herb salt. Sprinkle it on baked potatoes, soups, over a platter of scrambled eggs or on the top of poached fish. If you want to use it as a rub for grilled chicken, add just enough olive oil to moisten the ingredients and spread it inside the cavity and over the surface of the bird's skin. Allow the bird to marinate for 8 hours or overnight.

1 cup kosher or sea salt
2 tablespoons chopped dried orange peel
1 tablespoon chopped dried lemon peel
1 tablespoon dried rosemary
1 teaspoon dried lavender flowers
2 bay leaves, center ribs removed, crumbled

1 tablespoon toasted fennel seed
1 teaspoon toasted coriander seed
1 tablespoon coarsely ground black pepper
2 tablespoons dried oregano
2 tablespoons dried tarragon
3 tablespoons dried thyme

In a spice grinder, place 2 tablespoons of the salt, the orange and lemon peels, rosemary, lavender flowers, bay leaves, fennel and coriander seeds. Grind together until the peels are very small pieces. In a small bowl, combine this salt mixture with all the other ingredients. Store in a glass container in a cool, dark place.

Sage comes in a number of variegated or edged forms.

KOHLRABI

Brassica oleracea var. Gongylodes

Its hard to imagine that kohlrabi is related to the cabbage family, for its swollen stem appears to team it with root crops. The succulent, crunchy, rounded stem grows above ground, like a tennis ball sitting on top of the soil; leaves feather around the round bulb. Kohlrabi tastes much like cabbage and the leaf stems taste peppery, like radishes. Some of the heirloom types grow to 10 pounds, although most are harvested at the size of a softball or smaller. Its sweet crunchy texture makes kohlrabi a delicious treat.

Type

Biennial, grown as annual.

Size

Although some varieties grow to huge sizes, most kohlrabi are harvested once the bulbs have grown to 2 or 3 inches in diameter.

Kohlrabi is an unsung member of the cabbage family that's easy to grow.

Recommended Varieties

Don't be satisfied with growing just the green kohlrabi. Spice up the vegetable bed with purple or white kohlrabi—similar in flavor but great for variety. 'Grand Duke' is a reliable green hybrid, but purple 'Kolibri', with its purple skin and white flesh, is very handsome. Also look for 'Eder', a white kohlrabi that matures quickly.

When to Plant

Early in spring or mid-summer for a fall harvest. Some gardeners with early, hot summers find that kohlrabi only grows well for them in the fall.

Light

Full sun in coastal climate areas, some part shade in warm weather areas.

Soil

Humus-rich soil, kept moist during the growing season. Work in well-rotted compost and manure before planting.

How to Grow

Transplant seedlings or direct-sow early in spring, or mid-summer for fall harvest. Sow the seeds ½ inch deep and thin to 6 inches apart. Keep well watered during growth.

Propagation

By seed or by transplants. The seeds take up to 14 days to germinate.

Pests and Diseases

Enclose young plants with floating row covers to keep root maggots away. Spray the soil with Bt if you see cabbage moths fluttering around plants; they like kohlrabi as much as they do other cabbage family plants.

Give the "satellites" a humus-rich soil and plenty of water to keep them growing quickly.

Harvest

From 38 days for the earliest to 55 days for longer maturing varieties. Generally, harvest when globes are 2 to 3 inches in diameter. Trim off the leaves before storage.

Storage

Store in a plastic bag in the refrigerator crisper or place in a cool, dark place. Kohlrabi will store longer than other vegetables.

In the Kitchen

Use kohlrabi in place of radishes. Slice kohlrabi as chips for dip, grate it for coleslaw. Or, when the kohlrabi are the texture of carrots—still holding a bit of firmness but not raw tasting—make slices and toss with buttered herbs, then sauté.

Kohlrabi stores for up to 12 weeks in a root cellar if you keep temperatures between 33 and 40°F.

LETTUCE

Lactuca sativa

Lettuce does well in raised beds if you have well-drained soil. But don't let the soil dry out between waterings.

Butterhead lettuces form a loose head of tender leaves. Popular varieties include 'Dark Green Boston', 'Burpee Bibb', and 'Brune d'Hiver', which has a maroon tinge.

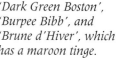

The early Greeks and Romans tossed salads, and their wandering armies carried the habit across Europe. As with plants so long in cultivation, many different varieties, both heirloom and hybrid, exist: There's a whole world beyond the common iceberg variety.

Lettuces grow in two different forms—those which make tight heads like iceberg or romaine varieties, and those which form loose clusters of leaves. The latter used to be called cutting lettuces, because their leaves could be cut individually over a period of time, instead of pulling out the whole head. Many heirloom lettuces are loose-leaf types with a uniquely shaped leaf such as 'Deer Tongue' or 'Oakleaf'; their superbly tender leaves wilt on trips any farther than from the garden to the kitchen.

Don't forget that lettuces look exceedingly handsome in flower beds. Plant in colorful designs alternating lime green-leafed types with bright red-leafed varieties. Use them as edible hedges or edging along walkways. Lettuces do well in containers, and teamed with scallions and pansies, the container becomes a complete salad bowl.

Type
Annual.

Size
Four to 12 inches tall.

Recommended Varieties
Grow as many types of lettuce in the garden as you can.

Heading lettuces like 'Crispino', Butterheads or Romaines can be lightly grilled if you don't use them as salad greens. Try also 'Salinas', 'Summertime', and especially the heirloom 'Rouge d'Hiver', a red-leafed romaine resistant to heat and cold. 'Little Gem' is a miniature romaine with excellent flavor and is small enough

Many forms and varieties of lettuce are definitely ornamental. You can grow them in mixed beds or containers.

'Ithaca' is a main-season head lettuce that resists tip burn.

to tuck between rows of beans or peas.

Harvest the outer leaves of loose leaf lettuces as you need them, extending their length of harvest. Heirloom loose-leaf varieties like 'Black-seeded Simpson', 'Oakleaf' and 'Deer Tongue' perform admirably, and are handsome enough to use in the flower border. Bolt-resistant Batavias are excellent for summer cultivation. Try 'Sierra', a bright red crisp-head lettuce.

When to Plant

Early spring and mid-summer for fall harvest. Some bolt-resistant types can stand summer heat, especially if they are planted so they are shaded against the afternoon sun. Seeds won't germinate when the temperatures exceed 80°F.

Light

Full sun to part shade, especially in the warmer growing seasons.

Soil

Humus-rich soil, kept moist during the growing season.

How to Grow

Seed or plant as early in the spring as soon the ground can

be worked. For the earliest harvest, start some seeds indoors six weeks before the last spring frost, then transplant young plants outside as soon as frost danger is past. Sow seeds ¼ inch deep and thin plants to 4 to 6 inches apart until their leaves touch. Then thin again, spacing plants 8 inches apart for small lettuces, 12 inches for large headed types.

Keep soil moist to avoid leaves becoming tough and bitter, or plants bolting. Sow a new patch of lettuce every three weeks to keep your salad bowl full of the freshest greens.

Propagation

Seed or transplants.

Pests and Diseases

Lettuce seedlings are vulnerable to slugs and snails as well as birds. Cover with portable mini-greenhouses or use row covers (secured by stones at the edges).

Harvest

50 to 65 days, depending upon variety. Tender thinnings can be added to salads, 3- to 4-inch plants can be harvested by the cut-and-come-again method (see page 98) or leave plants to mature. Harvest outer leaves of loose-leafed types. Wait to harvest heading lettuces until head has formed, but before the plant bolts. In hot weather, watch closely

In hotter climates, lettuce will need shade. Here, roofing shakes do the job.

as lettuces quickly bolt, making the leaves bitter tasting.

Storage

Loose-leafed lettuces do not store more than a day or two before turning yellow or melting into a green mess. Head lettuces will keep for 3 to 5 days maximum. Store in plastic bags in the crisper drawer of the refrigerator.

In the Kitchen

Salads, soups, wraps for fillings, wraps for grilled chicken or fish.

Other Uses

Try cooking lettuces, particularly iceberg. Stir-fry quickly like cabbage, or pair in the classic recipe of Spring Peas with Lettuce (below).

'Brunia' is a frilly and delicious oak-leaf lettuce.

Spring Peas with Lettuce

2 tablespoons butter
2 cups fresh podded peas (about 2 pounds unshelled)
2 cups iceberg lettuce leaves, torn in 2 inch pieces
¼ teaspoon dried thyme
1 tablespoon chive blossoms, optional
Salt and pepper to taste

Warm the butter in a sauté pan over medium heat. When the butter has melted, add the peas, shaking the pot while they cook for 2 to 4 minutes. Add the iceberg lettuce, thyme and chive blossoms. Season to taste. Cook for an additional minute to just wilt the lettuce, then serve.

Serves 4.

Mesclun Mixes
Lactuca sativa spp., *Brassica* spp.

Look for packets of mesclun mixes in seed catalogues or on nursery shelves. Some nurseries offer six-packs of mesclun seedlings ready to plant. These packets usually come with the seeds chosen for the most amenable blend of flavors and textures, matched to the same growing schedule. You may never have heard of greens like golden purslane, orach, amaranth and mizuna, but take heart—their easy cultivation plus great taste is only part of the joy of harvest.

Type
Annual.

Size
Varies according to mix. Plan to harvest when small and tender, about 2 to 3 inches tall.

Recommended Varieties
Early spring mixes are often labeled Asian Greens/Oriental Stir-Fry or piquant/spicy, for they contain types of mustards. Look for the spring lettuce mixes with lots of early season loose-leaf lettuces and greens. Summer mixes include heat resistant varieties, slower to bolt. Fall mixes, like

> ### TIP WINTER GREENS
> In a mild winter climate, you may have success growing mesclun in protected beds all winter long, although the leaves do toughen a bit with the cold, wet weather. If you have a south-facing bed underneath your house eaves, you may not even have to worry about frost. You can also make miniature greenhouses with plastic pipe bent into half moons to make tunnels over your beds to cover with plastic or Remay cloth. (On warm winter days, always leave the ends of the tunnels open to allow air to circulate.)

Mesclun mixes give you an attractive variety of colors, tastes and textures.

the early spring, will have lettuces and greens that can take the chilling weather.

When to Plant
Depends on mix. Be sure to plant the seeds designed for the season.

Light
Full sun, except in summer, when some shade is preferable.

Soil
Humus-rich soil, kept moist during the growing season. If you use the cut-and-come-again method, fertilize with a light application of fertilizer and compost after harvest to help the plants regrow.

How to Grow
Sow seeds or plants as soon as the ground can be worked in

the spring. Plant seeds ¼ inch deep, sowing thinly. If plants seem too densely packed, thin and use thinnings for salads. Keep soil moist to make sure leaves don't become tough and bitter or bolt. Sow a new patch of mesclun every three weeks.

Propagation
Seed or transplants.

Pests and Diseases
Mesclun seedlings are vulnerable to slugs and snails as well as birds. Cover with portable mini-greenhouses or use row covers.

Harvest
30 to 40 days, depending upon size of leaf desired. Add tender thinnings to salads. Harvest 3- to 4-inch plants by the cut-and-come-again method (page 98). Greens should grow back within 4 weeks for another cutting. Each plot should produce at least 3 to 4 harvests.

Harvest the young leaves and give them a rinse to remove dirt.

Storage

Mesclun lettuces do not store more than a day or two, in plastic bags in the refrigerator's crisper drawer.

In the Kitchen

Use the simplest salad dressing so the full flavor of the mesclun shines through.

Other Uses

Lightly-dressed greens can top pizza, or sprinkle finely-chopped greens on top of soup or sandwiches.

HARVEST METHOD: CUT-AND-COME-AGAIN

This harvesting technique, called "cut-and-come-again," uses a scissors or sharp knife.

When the leaves are about 2 inches or longer, start to harvest your mesclun. (Some of the greens toughen when their leaves are about 4 to 5 inches long.) Gently cut the plants about ½ to 1 inch above the soil line. Only cut as much as you need to fill your salad bowl.

Lightly fertilize and sprinkle with compost after harvest. Water regularly and let the plants grow back to the same size (about one month) to harvest again. Most types of mesclun can be harvested three or four times before you need to replant the bed.

Asian Greens
Brassica spp.

The Asian greens, members of the cabbage family, are used like lettuce when their leaves are young and tender. They grow vigorously. What makes them so attractive are the unusual shapes and colors of their leaves, and the pungent flavors that sing out. Unlike the delicate butter lettuces, which can only stand the subtlest of vinaigrettes, these greens stand up to flavored dressings. They add flavor and texture to meat, seafood or chicken salads. They also make superb wilted salads, with hot dressings.

Tatsoi or tah tsai looks like a rosette of spoon-shaped spinach leaves, but it's actually a mild mustard.

Type

Annuals. Mizuna is a biennial in warm-weather gardens.

Size

From 6-inch 'Tatsoi' to the 'Giant Red' mustard, topping out at 4 feet.

Recommended Varieties

'Red Giant' freely self-sows in garden beds, and comes up like self-sown flowers. The green leaves with their red stippling fills in empty spaces but can be easily weeded out when the space is needed. The mature plants can be a grandiose 4 feet tall with yellow edible flowers. Other varieties include:

Asian Stir-fry Blends: These grow quick and strong, but should be harvested before the leaves become too large—3 inches long at most.

Mizuna: A ferny green that adds textural beauty to a salad, but can also be stir-fried with garlic and balsamic vinegar. A biennial, it is slow to flower, but the flowers are edible.

Mustards: Strong-flavored mustards can be added to salads when small and cooked up as greens like collards when mature.

Pak Choi or Bok Choy: Both the sweet-flavored green leaves and the white tender stems are edible. Growing upright like cabbage, the outer leaves of pac choi can be harvested when they are 2 inches long, or the whole plant when it is 12 to 15 inches tall.

Tatsoi: One of the most delicious Asian greens—with a meaty leaf, appealing flavor and a silky texture. Harvest the young leaves for salad and steam or stir-fry the mature head.

'Osaka Purple' is a broadleaf mustard that can grow to 14 inches tall, but you can harvest the leaves when they're young for your salad mixes.

Baby bok choy adds tender leaves and crunchy midribs to salad mixes.

Red mustard leaves are zesty, and pretty too. As with most greens, you can harvest the outer leaves and let the inner ones develop.

When to Plant

Plant as soon as the ground can be worked in the spring and again in mid-summer for a fall harvest.

Light

Full sun, although these greens take part shade in the hottest part of the summer.

Soil

Humus-rich soil, kept moist during the growing season.

How to Grow

Sow seeds or plants as early in the spring as the ground can be worked. For early harvest, start seeds indoors six weeks before the last frost.

Propagation

Seed or transplants.

Pests and Diseases

Mesclun seedlings are vulnerable to slugs and snails as well as birds: cover with portable mini-greenhouses or use row covers.

Harvest

45 to 65 days, depending upon variety. Add tender thinnings to salads. Harvest 3- to 4-inch plants by the cut-and-come again method or leave plants to mature.

Storage

Leaves and mature plants are at their best for 3 to 5 days maximum. Store in plastic bags in the crisper drawer of the refrigerator.

In the Kitchen

Use the smallest leaves in salads. The larger leaves, with their bold and assertive flavors, can stand generous seasoning. Try them simmered with dried white beans for an Italian-style soup, or pair them with a ham bone and lentils.

Other Uses

Dry these greens and reconstitute in soups or long-simmering dishes. The texture is subtly altered by the drying.

Stir-Fried Asian Greens

1 tablespoon peanut or canola oil
1 clove garlic, finely chopped
1 knob fresh ginger, peeled and finely chopped
1 dried chile pepper, optional
4 cups coarsely chopped Asian greens
1 tablespoon soy sauce
1 teaspoon rice wine vinegar
¼ teaspoon salt
2 teaspoons toasted sesame seeds

In a wok or a sauté pan, heat the oil until it is quite hot. Add the garlic, ginger and chile. Cook for 30 seconds, stirring vigorously. Remove the chile and add the greens. Stir-fry for 2 to 3 minutes then pour in the soy sauce, the rice wine vinegar and the salt. Continue to stir-fry for an additional 2 to 3 minutes, or until the greens are tender. Turn out on a platter and sprinkle with the sesame seeds. Serve hot or at room temperature.

Serves 2.

Mizuna is a milder-flavored member of the mustard family.

Dandelion greens grown for the table.

The tight heads
of radicchio
yield beautiful leaves that spice up the
looks and the taste of any salad.

Exotic Greens

As American chefs travel abroad, they bring new foods home. Suddenly a salad looks like pieces of confetti, with bright red flashes of amaranth tossed with golden leaves of purslane. Peppery hot tastes of cress contrast with the cooling blandness of mache. Lemony-sour sorrel contrasts with the bitterness of dandelion, endive or escarole.

Many of these salad greens seem to grow by themselves. Simply sprinkle out the seed and stand back. Others (like endive) are more difficult to grow, but once it gets going, a perennial like sorrel can take over a garden.

Type

Annuals, with the exception of sorrel, which is a perennial.

Size

Varies according to plant.

Recommended Varieties

Arugula has become the darling of American chefs, turning up in dishes as diverse as salads, raviolis, sandwiches or soups. Once it establishes itself in the garden, it resows quite easily. The only compensation for its tendency to bolt are that the flowers are edible. Other exotic greens include:

Amaranth: (*Amaranthus* spp.) 35 to 40 days. Amaranth, which is related to the weed pigweed, grows as simply as its relative. Use the tasty leaves raw in salads or cooked like spinach. The brightly colored types in particular do well in the flower garden.

Arugula: (*Eruca sativa*) 30 to 40 days. Sometimes called rocket or roquette, this tasty salad green can be sautéed, pureed or made into soup. Try the heirloom variety—smaller with deeply cut leaves—*Eruca versicaria*, sometimes labeled as 'Italian Rustic' arugula. Arugula is fast growing, and reseeds easily.

Cress: (*Lepidium sativum*) 10 days. Curly cress, also known as pepper grass, grows quickly into a parsley-like plant with a clean, spicy taste. Sprout in water or grow for cut-and-come-again harvest.

Chervil: (*Anthriscus cereifolium*) 30 to 45 days. The flavors of parsley and anise blend in the ferny leaves of this 8-inch tall plant. Chervil prefers cooler temperatures and grows well in light shade.

Dandelion: (*Taraxacum officinalis*) 50 to 65 days. Not the garden variety of weed, this improved planting dandelion has wider leaves and a bold flavor.

Mâche: (*Valerianella locusta*) 35 to 45 days. Known as "Corn Salad," mâche makes rosettes of leaves in the garden, with buttery and nutty overtones in the salad

Chervil is a culinary herb of long standing that lends a light anise flavor to greens.

bowl. It only grows in cool seasons, and when summer heats up, its season is over.

Purslane: (*Portulaca oleracea*) 50 to 60 days. Unlike the common weed, cultivated purslane has large and succulent leaves which have a delicate flavor reminiscent of a lemon cucumber. 'Golden Purslane' is often an ingredient in mesclun mixes as it grows quickly and successfully.

Radicchio: (*Crichorium intybus*) 60 to 85 days. Radicchio comes in both red and green colors, and the slightly biting, bitter taste adds an interesting note when combined in salads, or grilled or baked in cream with Parmesan cheese. In mild winter gardens, plant in fall for spring harvest. In cold winter gardens, plant in May or early June.

Sorrel: (*Rumex acetosa*) One of the first perennials to leaf out in the spring with lemony,

Endive or frisee is a close relative of radicchio. The finely cut, curly leaves distinguish it from escarole, which has flatter leaves.

Grilled Greens

Grilled greens taste smoky and rich. For a sharper flavor, substitute a vinaigrette in place of the sesame oil.

4 cups washed radicchio heads, cut in half
2 tablespoons soy sauce
1 teaspoon white wine or rice vinegar

2 tablespoons sesame oil
¼ teaspoon salt
½ teaspoon freshly ground pepper

Toss the greens with the soy sauce, vinegar, sesame oil, salt and pepper. Place over a moderately hot grill, turning every 30 seconds so the greens brown but do not burn. Serve immediately after the greens are warmed through and lightly browned.

Serves 4.

'Red Treviso' radicchio is a reliable heirloom from Italy.

tart leaves. The French make soups, sauces and salads with sorrel. Or use like a grape leaf to wrap fish for poaching.

When to Plant

As early in the spring as the ground can be worked. In mid-summer for fall harvest.

Light

Sun with some afternoon shade, particularly later in spring.

Soil

Humus-rich soil, kept moist during the growing season.

How to Grow

Sow seeds or plants in beds as early in the spring as the ground can be worked. You can start some seeds indoors six weeks before the last spring frost. Thin plants to 2 to 4 inches apart. If plants seem too thick, thin and use for salads. Keep the soil

Mâche or corn salad will take cold temperatures, so you can plant it early in the season or late in the fall and still get nice harvests.

moist. Resow in mid-summer for fall crops.

Propagation

Seed or transplants.

Pests and Diseases

Seedlings are vulnerable to slugs, snails and birds. Protect plants with portable mini-greenhouses or row covers.

Harvest

30 to 40 days, depending upon size of leaf desired. Add tender thinnings to salads. Harvested by

the cut-and-come-again method (page 98) or leave plants to mature.

Storage

Use immediately. If necessary, place in plastic bags and store for 1 to 2 days in the refrigerator crisper drawer.

In the Kitchen

Make fresh salads with the tender sweet cuttings. Use the simplest salad dressing so the full flavor of the greens shines through. Sturdier greens can be sautéed or grilled. Sorrel is famous as the basis for a sauce often used with fish or chicken. Use lightly dressed greens to top pizza, or finely chop them and sprinkle on soup or sandwiches.

Other Uses

The variegated 'Jacob's Coat' and the ornamental amaranth, 'Love-Lies-Bleeding', make handsome flower garden plants.

Arugula is easy to grow in a short time—30 to 40 days—and has dozens of uses in the kitchen.

Belgian endive, another member of the chicory family, can be forced from the roots to produce tight cylindrical heads.

MELONS

Cucumis melo and *Citrullus lanatus*

The sweet, fragrant taste of melons signals that summer is at its height. Melons can be divided into two groups: the muskmelons (with a netted skin), *C. melo* var. *reticulatus*; and the casaba or honeydew melons, *C. melo* var. *inodorus*, which have smooth green skin and can be green- or pink-fleshed.

Of a different texture and flavor is the watermelon (*Citrullus lanatus*). Originating in Africa, watermelons are related to cucumbers and have many of the same cultural requirements. They can be cantaloupe-sized, about 1 pound each, or gargantuan 40-pounders. Although the largest melons like a long season of heat both day and night, the small icebox mel-

ons, maturing in 75 to 80 days, do well in cooler summer climates.

If your temperatures are on the cool side, regardless of the melons you are raising, increase the soil temperature for added success: Spread black plastic on top of the ground around the melon plants.

Type
Annuals.

Size
Vines can stretch for 6 to 8 feet.

Recommended Varieties
Recommending muskmelons is almost a dangerous act, because each variety is so sensitive

The melon family accounts for scores of colors, shapes, sizes and flavors.

Cantaloupe wrapped in proscuitto is the real deal in Italian cuisine.

'Moon and Stars' watermelon is out of this world.

Two watermelons with good storage qualities are 'Winter King' and 'Winter Queen'. Some folks can serve fresh watermelon at Thanksgiving dinner.

Watermelon Salad

Watermelon salad can be addicting. Actually, it crosses the line between salad and salsa with its cool-and-hot, sweet-and-sour balances. Add more spice to the salad if you wish. Serve it at the side of grilled chicken or meat as a salsa, or as a salad accompanying sandwiches.

4 cups watermelon, seeded, and cubed in 1-inch squares or in large melon balls
¼ cup finely diced red onion
1 tablespoon finely chopped basil
1 tablespoon finely chopped mint
¼ teaspoon cayenne pepper, or to taste
1 tablespoon mild-flavored olive oil
1 teaspoon white wine vinegar
Salt and freshly ground pepper to taste

Toss all the ingredients together. Adjust the seasonings to what you and your guests will like. Keep chilled until serving.

Serves 4.

to each climate. 'Charantais'—imported from France—is one variety that is universally applauded. 'Charantais' is spoken about in hushed reverence—their perfumed fragrance and silky flesh are extraordinary. The early maturing 'Alienor', 'Charmel' and 'Flyer' are other charantais hybrids offered in catalogs. But don't stop there: try the short season cantaloupe 'Galia', or the 'Early Sugarshaw', a hybrid that can weigh up to 8 pounds and is known for its pink flesh and rich flavor.

'Earli-dew', a honeydew melon, has been bred for short-season growth and is resistant to fusarium wilt. It is perfect for cool summer locations.

When deciding on watermelon types, look for the small, sweet icebox melons no bigger than 2 pounds and with yellow instead of pink flesh. Large (25 to 40 pound) watermelons require lots of nitrogen-rich soil, endless gallons of water, and a long, warm growing season.

When to Plant

In spring, after the last chance of frost has passed and when the nights do not fall below 50°F. If you prefer, start the seeds indoors four to six weeks before the last frost.

Light

Full sun.

Soil

Rich, well-drained soil with plenty of well-rotted manure and compost worked in at least 2 weeks before planting.

How to Grow

For hill planting, mound the prepared soil to form a round bed that is 2 feet in diameter

'Savor' is a charantais-type melon that has to be grown in the home garden for the best flavor.

TIP MELON MANIA

Although any melon is delicious eaten out of hand, try freezing seeded melon squares to make smoothies or a sorbet in a blender. The refreshing crunch of watermelon cools off fiery hot salsas. Thick-skinned watermelons have long been used to make sweet watermelon rind pickles.

Watermelons come in all sizes—from 2 to 40 pounds—and many flesh colors, including red, white, pink, yellow and orange.

and about 6 inches higher than the normal soil level. Leave 6 feet between hills. Sow 6 seeds on each hill, pushing them down 1 inch deep. Pat the soil down firmly. Thin to the three strongest seedlings when they are 3 inches high.

Keep the soil moist but not soggy. Mulch plants with 3 inches of organic compost. In cool summer climates, use a black plastic mulch over the compost to boost temperatures. Melons can be trellised using wire or netting, to help the vines grow upward. Use soft cotton strips to support developing fruit in "hammocks."

Propagation

Seed or transplants. The melon family cross-pollinates easily, so any seed-saving must be done carefully—hand pollinating flowers and then tying up blooms to prevent any additional pollination from wind or insects. To save the seeds of open-pollinated types, collect, wash and dry them for about three to five days, then store.

HEIRLOOM MELONS

Part of the fun of growing heirlooms comes with the aura of romance they bring to the garden. 'Moon & Stars' watermelons bring an image of the night sky down to the ground. Instead of the familiar two-toned green rind, 'Moon & Stars' offers a deep, dark, night-green sky accented by polka dots, golden moons and smaller pinpoints of stars. It is available with yellow or red flesh; both have a sweet, rich flavor that makes a 25-pound melon disappear quickly.

For the best vine-ripened flavor, harvest cantaloupes when the stem separates from the fruit.

Pests and Diseases

Striped cucumber beetles can damage plants. Hand pick to remove them. Melons are susceptible to powdery mildew. Water plants by drip irrigation or at ground level. Also, choose mildew-resistant varieties.

Harvest

To intensify flavor and keep the melons from splitting, reduce watering as fruit approach ripeness.

Pick melons only when they are ripe—they will not ripen well off the vine. Pick when the tendril nearest the stem shrivels and when the melon slips off the stem. For watermelons, look at the bottom of the melon: A color change from dark green to lighter yellow indicates ripeness. Also examine the tendrils next to the stem—when they shrivel, the melon is ripe.

Storage

Don't refrigerate melons. Keep them at room temperature and eat them as soon as possible. Watermelons will hold 5 to 7 days if kept in a cool, dark place.

In the Kitchen

Eat melons fresh, still warm from the sun, puréed for cold melon soup, or frozen to make sorbets. Melon wrapped with proscuitto is a unique summer first course.

Other Uses

Try melons as ingredients in a spicy salsa: a great side to grilled meats.

A homegrown watermelon sliced on the patio is an all-American treat.

Basil Syrup for Fresh Melons

Although you might not think of combining basil with a sugar syrup for melons, the flavor actually makes the perfect complement. Try the syrup with other fruits as well.

2 cups water
1 cup sugar
20 basil leaves

Heat the water and sugar together until the sugar dissolves completely. Add the basil leaves and remove from heat. Let the syrup steep for 1 hour, covered in the refrigerator. Remove the basil leaves and pour over cut melon pieces. Serve within two hours.

OKRA

Abelmoschus esculentus

The best flavor comes from okra pods that are picked soft and young—at about 2 inches long.

Pickled okra adds an exotic accent to a cool summer beverage.

Okra came to America from Africa, probably as a result of the slave trade in the 1660s.

Okra is a member of the mallow family. The yellow flowers that grow along the stem are quite lovely. Some varieties stretch up to 7 feet tall, while dwarf varieties only grow 2 to 3 feet tall. The pods of the heirloom 'Cow Horn' or the Asian 'Burmese' grow up to 12 inches long. But most gardeners pick the pods at about 3 inches to keep them sweet and tender.

For people who were raised in the South, okra is comfort food: rich gumbos with slices of okra, okra fritters and crisp okra pickles. When okra is cooked by people unfamiliar with its characteristics it may turn into a sticky and gummy concoction. If cooked correctly, okra emerges as a tender and sweet vegetable. When sliced and cooked, okra thickens stews and gumbos. It holds its shape and tastes somewhat like green beans.

One pod is not fancy to look at, but okra is a versatile vegetable in the kitchen. Try growing it as an offbeat ornamental in a container.

Pick young okra pods daily to keep the plant producing more fruit.

Lightly sautéed okra, cooled and dressed with a little oil, is a delicious summer salad.

Type
Annual.

Size
3½ to 7 feet tall.

Recommended Varieties
First-time growers should try a couple of rows of 'Clemson Spineless' or 'Cajun Delight', both old favorites which grow 4 to 5 feet tall. 'Burgundy' is a newer selection; it has red-colored pods and grows only to about 3 to 4 feet. 'Annie Oakley' produces well in cool summer climates, so no one has the excuse they can't grow okra.

When to Plant
When the soil warms in the spring and when night temperatures do not fall below 50°F.

Light
Full sun.

Soil
Loose, fertile, loamy soil. Work generous amounts of compost into clay soil.

How to Grow
Start seeds inside 4 to 6 weeks before the last frost. Plant in individual pots, because young seedlings do not like to have their roots disturbed. In long summer climates, sow seed directly, ¾ to 1 inch deep, when soil warms. Seeds emerge in 7 to 14 days. Space plants every 12 to 15 inches depending upon variety. Keep watered and mulch well as the season progresses.

Okra adds a colorful touch to the garden with its bright pods and showy flowers.

Propagation
Seed, or carefully transplant seedlings grown in individual pots.

Pests and Diseases
Hardy, with few diseases or pests.

Harvest
55 to 60 days to harvest. Pick okra pods when they are small and tender—about 2 to 3 inches long. Okra flowers are edible as well. Traditionally, the seeds were dried, toasted and ground as a coffee substitute.

Storage
Fresh okra spoils quickly. Pick and cook within one or two days. You can pickle, freeze or dry to preserve for winter use.

In the Kitchen
Quickly sauté small, whole pods in butter, slice and cook in gumbos, or make into fritters. Small pods can be pickled like green beans.

TIP   OKRA TIP

Okra seeds are very hard. Soaking the seeds overnight speeds germination. You can also sand the seeds slightly.

ONIONS

Globe Onion, *Allium cepa* and Bunching Onion, *Allium fistulosum*

Chives give you lots of fresh leaves for salads and other kitchen uses, plus nice flowers for an ornamental touch.

Delicious shallots are a form of multiplier onion, setting clusters of 6 to 12 cloves.

'Red Torpedo' is a variety best grown for fresh slicing.

The *Allium* family has been cultivated for the flavor of its bulbs and leaves. Around 2300 B.C., the Sumarians ate wheat and barley, chickpea and lentils spiced with onions, garlic and leeks. Egyptian papyrus rolls list purchases of onions for the workers on the pyramids. Nomadic tribes cultivated wild onions and many different varieties were spread from country to country. More varieties came to America when immigrants came to America.

Onion growth is affected by the length of days. Consequently, some onions grow better in the South, while others do better in the North. The term "long-day" refers to onions that need longer daylight to bulb fully, while short-day onions grow better with less. Most catalog houses set the border in a line between San Francisco and Nashville, so gardeners north of the line grow long-day; those south, short-day. Some bulbs are less sensitive and will grow well in all locations.

Type

Biennials, grown as annuals. But "Egyptian" or "top setting" onions, *Allium cepa proliferatum*, are grown as perennials.

Size

From 12 inches to 24 inches tall, depending upon variety.

Recommended Varieties

Today, the most common type of onion is the globe onion in varieties colored white, yellow and purple. Try 'Walla Walla'—a variety that grows well in every region. A recent import from Italy is the 'Cippollini' onion. It has a flattened disk shape and a sweet flavor. To add color to your dish, try 'Italian Torpedo' but eat them quickly because they don't store well.

The globe onion has more relatives including leeks. Try the new 'Albinstar Baby' leek, harvested at a mere ½ inch in diameter. You'll also want to try chives, shallots and

Onions come in many different forms, flavors and keeping qualities.

ONIONS AS FLOWERS?

Use the onion family in the flower garden! Society garlic (*tulbeghia violacea*) is an ornamental, variegated, grass-like plant with edible pink flowers. Chives—both the small-leafed, pink-flowering kind and the broader-leafed Chinese chives—accent flower gardens with tufts of upright, spear-like leaves. Pick the onion-fragrant leaves to top soups, vinaigrettes, salads and of course, baked potatoes.

Garlic chives (Allium tuberosum) *are perennials in Zones 4 to 8. They can become a weed if left to ramble.*

Egyptian or top-setting onions are a perennial plant. The bulblets at the top of the plant multiply when they "walk" or touch the ground. They also produce underground bulb clusters.

multiplier onions. Multiplier onions, like garlic and shallots, form a bunch or cluster of onions around the single planted bulb.

When to Plant

As early in spring as soon as the ground can be worked. Start seeds inside 4 weeks before the last frost and transplant into the garden.

You can grow lots of onions in a small space. Most bulbing types can be grown 3 to 4 inches apart.

Light

Full sun.

Soil

Onions are not deep rooted, therefore the top 8 inches of soil should be well-worked with compost and well-rotted manure. The soil pH should be between 6 and 7.

How to Grow

Plant seeds ¼ inch deep or sets 1 to 2 inches deep, sowing thickly in rows 12 to 14 inches apart. As onions grow, thin for kitchen use, ending with onions about 3 or 4 inches apart. Keep the beds weeded and the soil moist but not soggy. Use a mulch to help maintain moisture and keep weeds down. Do not cut

TIP — GRILLED HOMEGROWN LEEKS

Pull leeks to thin the row when plants are pencil-sized. Brush the harvested leeks with olive oil and grill quickly over red-hot charcoal.

tops at any period as this will deter bulb growth.

Propagation

Seeds, dried bulbs or onion transplants.

Pests and Diseases

Plant varieties resistant to pink root disease. Use floating

Leeks from the garden taste better than the bland ones in the grocery store. Try growing a row of them and you'll be convinced.

Plant onion sets 3 to 6 inches apart, depending on the size of the mature bulb.

row covers to keep onion maggots away.

Harvest

From 50 days to 300 (for over-wintering onions in mild-winter climates) to harvest, depending upon variety. When tops start to dry and fall over, stop watering. After half of the tops have fallen over, push over the rest. Let the onions cure in the soil for a week, then harvest. Dry in filtered shade.

Storage

Some onions do not store for very long. Store cured onions in a dark, cool place. If available, store in hanging onion sacks (like mesh bags for oranges). You can also braid onions. Check periodically and remove any softened onions. It is best not to store onions in the refrigerator.

In the Kitchen

Onions can be pickled, grilled, baked and used as seasoning for just about everything.

Other Uses

Dry onion slices to use as seasoning, grinding to a coarse powder with salt.

'Borettana' (also called 'Cipollini') onions are an Italian heirloom that's great for pickling or grilling.

Harvest bulbs whenever they're large enough to use. They're mature when the leaves turn yellow. These are being harvested just before total maturity.

Red onions can be sweet or pungent, but they're indispensible for salads, burgers, grilling and dozens of other uses.

TIP

USE IMMEDIATELY

Once sliced or chopped, the cut surfaces of onions begin to oxidize, producing an off-flavor and a kind of rank odor. Cook onions as soon as sliced. If that is not possible, cover the cut onions with water or vinegar until used. When covered with water, some of the "heat" of the onion will be dispersed, useful with long stored onions or overly strong onions.

PARSNIPS

Pastinaca sativa

Parsnips have languished because they haven't been rediscovered by current food fads. Yet they feature equally with other vegetables in *Chez Panisse Vegetables*, by Alice Waters, one of the best chefs in America.

Before the discovery of the potato, the parsnip held an important position as a major winter food because it stores in the ground regardless of frost or snow, and actually sweetens after the first frosts. Growing parsnips, like carrots, guarantees a supply of root crops for winter. Add as a sweetener to mashed potatoes. Fry like potatoes to tender crisps, or cube and roast in a melange of carrots, potatoes, beets and turnips.

Type

Biennial, grown as an annual.

Size

Root crop, requiring spacing of 2 to 3 inches between plants.

Recommended Varieties

There is not a great deal of choice with parsnips: 'Hollow Crown' is an heirloom variety grown in the nineteenth century. 'Lancer' is a newer variety.

When to Plant

Mid- to late summer for harvest after the first frosts.

Light

Full sun.

Parsnips need a long growing season to fully develop. Grow them in a loose soil with good drainage.

Soil

Light, friable soil to allow the roots to develop, much the same as carrots. Do not over fertilize because rich soil causes parsnips to fork and grow hairy.

TIP A DIFFERENT KIND OF WINE

Parsnip wine used to be offered to guests as an elegant treat.

Parsnips can be grown almost anywhere in North America. They're hardy to Zone 2.

Bubbe's Chicken Soup

A beloved Bubbe (Grandma) shared her chicken soup recipe with us. The parsnips add interesting crunch and a snap of flavor when you bite into them. This chicken soup is the real thing—the kind that will make you feel better no matter what's ailing you.

1 large chicken, cut up
2 qts. (approximate) cold water
1 onion quartered
3 stalks celery cut in large chunks, including tops
Sprigs of parsley
3 carrots, scraped and cut in large chunks at an angle
3 parsnips, scraped and cut in thick slices
Salt
White pepper
Poultry seasoning
3 cloves garlic, coarsely chopped
} All to taste (You'll get a feel for the right amount)

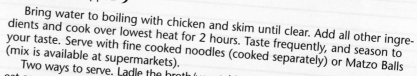

Bring water to boiling with chicken and skim until clear. Add all other ingredients and cook over lowest heat for 2 hours. Taste frequently, and season to your taste. Serve with fine cooked noodles (cooked separately) or Matzo Balls (mix is available at supermarkets).

Two ways to serve. Ladle the broth/vegetables over the noodles or matzo and eat as a soup, then use the chicken in sandwiches afterward or make chicken salad. Or, pull the meat from the bones and just have your chicken right in the soup.

How to Grow

Seeds usually take about 3 to 4 weeks to germinate, so keep the soil moist during the germination period. Germination can be quite light, so sow heavily. Keep rows or beds well weeded and thin to 2 to 3 inches apart.

Propagation

Sow seed directly into the ground.

Pests and Diseases

Parsnips have few pest problems. Rotate your location every year for healthier crops.

In the Kitchen

Cook as you would carrots or combine with potatoes. Baked in combination with other winter vegetables, parsnip adds a sweet touch. Parsnips make a great addition to soups and stews with their tart flavor and crunchy bite. Poach or steam until tender or deep fry in a fritter batter. Some cooks treat parsnips like pumpkins and make soup, or create a puree as a side to meat dishes.

Harvest

110 to 120 days. Wait to harvest until after several nights of frost sweeten the roots. Harvest in fall and leave some crop to harvest in the early spring when the ground first thaws.

Storage

Leave in the ground and pull when you are ready to cook, or harvest after the first frosts and store in a cool, dark place.

Parsnips are more versatile than they're generally regarded. Try cooking them like carrots.

PEAS

Pisum sativum

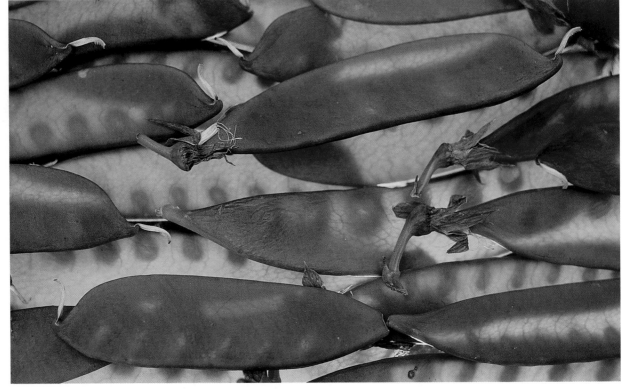

Snow peas should be harvested young—before the peas swell and the pods become tough.

A harbinger of spring! Sweet and tender peas are best grown in the garden and taken straight to the kitchen because their sugars begin turning to starch the moment they are picked. English peas must be shelled out of their tough pods, but

Garden or English peas give us those wonderful fresh peas. 'Thomas Laxton' and 'Lincoln' are two heirlooms.

Oriental snow peas and sugar snap peas are eaten pod and all.

The growing tips of pea vines, the tendrils, can also be harvested when the stems are no more than ¼ inch thick. Sauté to bring out their intense pea flavor.

English peas like the moist and cool weather of early spring, but the snow and snap peas will last until summer warms days and nights. Because the sweetness of peas is so perishable, homegrown peas offer a distinct advantage to store bought. Some types now grow on bush-type plants while others require staking.

Type
Annual.

Size
From 2-foot self-standing vines (dwarf types) to 4½- to 5-foot tall vines.

Recommended Varieties

For shelling peas, try the earliest 'Alaska' or 'Maestro', disease-resistant varieties which some gardeners prefer for fall planting. For edible-podded peas, the 'Dwarf Gray Sugar' grows manageable, 2-foot-tall

A LITTLE PLANNING

Dwarf-type peas tend to produce pods all at once—great for freezing but less useful for meals. Sow dwarf types successively to prolong the harvest. Or plant a combination of dwarf for freezing and vine for home cooking.

New varieties of peas are sweeter than ever. Eat them fresh for the best taste.

vines with edible pink flowers. Try 'Sugar Ann', the quickest growing of all the snap peas on a bush. 'Super Sugar Snap' provides both edible pod or shelled peas, whichever you wish, but the 5-foot-tall vines need support.

When to Plant

In cool weather. However, prolonged, wet ground may rot the seed so reseed as necessary. Plant in early spring or 10 weeks before first fall frost.

Light

Full sun in cool weather, some shade for edible pod peas in early or late summer.

Soil

Soil should be more alkaline than acidic, with a pH of 6 to 7. Garden inoculant can be added to the soil to introduce bacteria that

Eons better than canned or frozen store-bought peas, fresh shelled peas say "delicious" in any kitchen.

help plant roots absorb more nitrogen which improves growth. To assure this form of cooperation, purchase an inoculant powder, which is actually the bacteria in a dried form. Moisten the seeds and sprinkle inoculant over the top; plant the sprinkled seeds immediately.

How to Grow

Use cut brush stuck in the ground as staking, or provide netting or wire for the young plants to climb up on. Provide consistent moisture. Water at ground level to prevent powdery mildew in the summer months.

Propagation

Seed or transplant seedlings.

Pests and Diseases

Plant varieties resistant to blight, wilt and mildew. If birds are a problem, throw netting over your plants.

Harvest

50 to 60 days. English peas should fill the pod but still be small and tender. Harvest snow peas when pods are still flat, be-

---

TIP **WARNING**

Blooms of flowering sweet peas, the ornamental, are *not* edible.

---

fore peas form. Sugar snap peas snap like beans when ready, and are plump and rounded.

Storage

Harvest just before cooking or preserving.

In the Kitchen

Peas, pods and pea tendrils can be eaten in salads or quickly sautéed or stir-fried. Warning: the sweet fresh taste vanishes when overcooked. Snow peas and sugar snap peas must have their strings removed before cooking: Snap off the top and tail of the peas, pulling off the string along the long end.

Other Uses

All pods can be frozen. Harvest tendrils to use fresh in salads. Stir-fry tendrils too.

Sugar snap peas are eaten pod and all. 'Sugar Ann' and 'Sugar Snap' have both won All America Selections awards.

Pea-Vine Tendril Salad

We are not used to eating the tendrils, but they are full of pea flavor and sweet and tender to boot. Some of your wilder growing vines can stand a bit of pruning to add to the salad bowl.

4 cups mesclun
2 cups pea tendrils, about 2 inches long
Blossoms of 'Dwarf Gray', optional

2 tablespoons fruity olive oil
2 teaspoons white wine vinegar
Salt and pepper to taste

In a salad bowl, toss together the mesclun, pea tendrils and blossoms, if available. In a small bowl, whip together the oil and vinegar. Toss the salad with the dressing, then salt and pepper to taste. Serve immediately.

Serves 4.

PEPPERS

Capsicum annuum

Colorful peppers add zest to the eye as well as the tastebuds.

Pepper heat ranges from an ultimate fiery fury that seems to etch a hole right through your tongue, to the cool and sweet crunch of bell peppers.

Relatives of tomatoes and eggplants, peppers have more than five times as much vitamin C as tomatoes. Many people dislike green bell peppers, and with good reason. These immature peppers are often bitter and, like green fruit, can cause digestive upset. Ripe peppers may have tougher skins, and should be peeled.

To peel, blacken the surface of peppers over a charcoal fire, on a gas burner, or under a broiler. Immediately place the peppers or chiles into a closed container or plastic bag and let steam. When cool, skins will peel off easily. Do not wash the peppers or you will lose the smoky flavor.

Type

Perennials, grown as annuals.

Size

One to 3 feet.

Recommended Varieties

Sweet peppers are so good you'll want to plant a variety of them. Try 'Hungarian Sweet Wax', a long yellow type. Add 'Sweet Chocolate' (brown), 'Secret' (purple), and a red, meaty pimiento such as 'Apple' or 'Figaro'. For hot chile peppers, the tiny 'Thai Dragon' will set tongues aflame.

When to Plant

After days and nights warm and night temperatures don't drop below 50°F.

Light

Full sun.

'Anaheim' peppers are perfect for chiles rellenos. Individual bushes or fruits can vary in their degree of hotness (if any), but 'Anaheim' never gets fiery.

Soil

Nitrogen-rich soil encourages peppers to grow leaves, not blooms. Peppers require quantities of potassium and phosphorous with only medium amounts of nitrogen. Work in quantities of well-rotted compost.

How to Grow

Start seeds inside; set them ½ inch deep. They take 14 days to germinate. Then set plants 12 to 18 inches apart in rows 30 inches apart. Use a low-nitrogen fertilizer. Water consistently.

'Gypsy' is an All America Selections winner with a sweet taste. Plants have tolerance of tobacco mosaic virus.

A basketful of pungent-to-downright-hot peppers (clockwise from top): 'Fresno', 'Del Arbol', 'Anaheim', 'Cascabella', 'Serrano', 'Pasilla' and 'Jalapeño' (center).

 TIP RIPE IS BETTER

Green peppers are really not-yet-ripe peppers, but we have learned to eat them for the convenience of their long-keeping. Ripen your peppers to their full colors before harvesting.

Refrigerator Pickled Peppers

Everyone knows that Peter Piper picked a peck of pickled peppers, so try these out on your household.

20 peppers, either whole or sliced in 1-inch wide pieces
4 cloves garlic
2 bay leaves
2 cups white or white wine vinegar
1 cup water
2 teaspoons sugar
1 tablespoon pickling salt

Prepare peppers, washing and drying them. Divide the garlic, bay, and peppers between two jars. If necessary to fill jars, add more peppers.

In a small pan, mix together the vinegar, water, sugar and salt—heat to boiling. Stir until salt and sugar have dissolved.

Pour the liquid into the two jars. If the jars are not quite filled, add vinegar to bring level ½ inch below the rim of the jar. Seal the jars and store in the refrigerator. Pickles are ready to eat after 1 week. They will keep in the refrigerator for up to 3 months.

Makes 2 quart jars of pickles.

HOT! USE CAUTION!

Use extreme caution when handling spicy hot peppers. Many cooks use rubber gloves when deseeding or peeling blackened peppers. Avoid touching your eyes or other tender areas until you have thoroughly washed your hands to remove any vestige of the capsaicin oil, which irritates and burns skin.

'Habanero' peppers (Capsicum chinense) *are at the top of the heat scale. Handle with care!*

When plants are 8 inches high, cover with 3 to 4 inches of mulch. To encourage root development, pull off flowers for the first month the plant is in the ground. Many peppers grow well in containers.

Propagation

Seed or transplant seedlings.

Pests and Diseases

If you have a problem with soil-borne diseases, use resistant varieties and rotate crops regularly; avoid locations where eggplants or tomatoes grew the previous year.

 TIP **CHILL OUT**

Peppers don't have to be blanched before freezing. Just wash thoroughly, dry, cut up and store in freezer bags.

Harvest

Harvest when peppers have begun to show color, or let fully color for drying. To dry small peppers, pull up the whole plant and hang upside down in a dry and hot location, such as a porch.

Storage

Store up to 5 days in plastic bags in the refrigerator crisper.

In the Kitchen

Use raw in salads, sauté for stir-fry or as an addition to soups and stews. Stuff small, seeded jalapeños with a cream cheese or bean spread for spicy hors d'oeuvres. Stuff large bells with a meat or vegetarian filling for entrées. Jalapeños stuffed with garlic and pickled make a great "olive" for martinis.

'Fresno', a Mexican import, is a medium-hot pepper that turns red.

'Diablo Grande' is a medium-hot pepper.

Most peppers develop their best taste when they turn from green to their mature color. Frequent harvests keep the plants producing new fruit.

POTATOES

Solanum tuberosum

Nowadays the home gardener can grow dozens of potatoes in different sizes, colors, and textures.

Discovered in Peru in the 16th century, potatoes are related to peppers, tomatoes and eggplants—all members of the *Solanaceae* family. There are some 13,000 types of potatoes known today, and some 2,000 varieties are commonly grown all over the world— from the hot, humid, seaside plots of the Philippines to the cool, cloud-high Andes Mountains.

In the late 1500s, Sir Walter Raleigh was given strange tubers. He planted them on his farms in Ireland. The potatoes grew easily in the rocky Irish soil, out-producing the grains that were the primary food for animals and people at that time.

The Irish brought the potato back to the New World, specifically the immigrants who settled and farmed in Londonderry, New Hampshire in 1719.

Back in Ireland, potatoes quickly replaced grain as a diet staple for the Irish peasant. Potatoes had an unfinicky growing habit and sturdy nutritional qualities, so this is no suprise.

But only one potato variety was grown, so when fungal diseases struck in 1845, the entire potato crop failed, creating a great famine. One million people in Ireland died between 1846 and 1851.

A potato harvest can look like an Easter egg basket with spuds in shades of yellow, pink, blue and purple. Potatoes are rich in vitamins and minerals, low in fat and calories. New red or pink potatoes are best boiled or grilled. White, yellow and purple potatoes take well to boiling or baking.

Type
Annual.

Size
Potato plants grow 3 to 4 feet tall, with gangly branches.

'Red Lasoda' is an early-season variety that does well in both the South and the North. It's a good keeper too.

COMPOST-PILE POTATOES

Because potatoes love loose soil, some gardeners grow potatoes in a compost pile 3 feet high.

First, create a compost heap with 6-inch concrete reinforcing wire circled and fastened so the diameter is at least 36 inches wide.

Starting in the fall, load all your leaves and green compost into the wire circle. In the early spring plant potatoes 4 inches under the top of the compost pile, and continue adding organic matter to the heap.

The sprouts grow up through the compost surrounded in the kind of medium they most enjoy. After potatoes have been harvested, pull apart the compost pile, toss and apply to your garden beds.

If you're crowded for space, try growing potatoes in a thick trash bag. Use a rich soil mix and keep the plants well-watered. You could reap 10 to 20 pounds per bag.

Recommended Varieties

There is nothing more delicious than tiny pink potatoes pulled out of the soil and popped into the pot! 'Dark Red Norland' is an early variety with fine flavor. The gold flesh of 'Yukon Gold' looks lovely and is full of flavor—a must in any garden. Try the fingerlings such as 'Giant Peanut'. For variety, try purple potatoes: 'All Blue' is a good one to mash as a shocking dish to serve your guests.

When to Plant

After the last chance of frost in the spring. In mild-winter areas, plant a fall crop to over-winter and harvest in the spring.

Light

Full sun.

Soil

The potato loves a loose, compost-rich bed, so prepare your soil 12 inches deep with generous amounts of compost and mulch well with partially decomposed leaves or straw. Add a timed-release, pelleted plant food when turning the soil, preferably one with low nitrogen (formulated for tomatoes) so the plant produces tubers and not just greenery.

Cut larger seed potatoes into pieces with one or two "eyes." Let the pieces cure for a day or so. Smaller seed potatoes can be planted whole. Always use certified disease-free seed potatoes.

Potato blossoms are pretty. Notice the similarity to the flowers of eggplants, peppers and tomatoes? They're all relatives in the nightshade family.

Plant your seed potatoes about 12 inches apart in rich, humusy, acidic soil.

Blue-fleshed potatoes can give a wakeup call to the table. They're great for mashing.

How to Grow

The classic method is trench planting. New potatoes form above the original planted tuber so you want to plant tubers deep enough to allow room for lots of new potatoes to grow on top of the planted potato chunk. Dig a trench 8 inches deep and work in a low nitrogen fertilizer (such as one formulated for tomatoes) at the same time. Add the potato pieces, with the eyes facing up and each chunk spaced about 14 inches apart. Fill the trench with 4 inches of soil or compost. Pat the soil down firmly and water thoroughly. When the sprouts grow up, add another 4 inches of soil and don't worry if you cover some of the sprouts. As the sprouts grow up again, add one last 4-inch layer of compost or soil to make a hill. Water thoroughly after each addition of compost or soil.

Propagation

Locate certified seed potatoes either at your nursery or through catalogs; these are disease free and have not been treated to retard sprouting.

The surface of a potato is pocked with dimples—known as "eyes." Cut up your tubers so there are one or two eyes to each piece. Small potatoes can be planted uncut.

Pests and Diseases

Early or late potato blight can hit potatoes. Besides buying certified seed potatoes, water at the base of the plants early in the day so the water does not sit on the leaves overnight.

Roasted potatoes and onions with rosemary.

Harvest

Sixty days for baby potatoes, to 90 days or more for full size; depending on variety. To harvest potatoes, watch for plants to produce five-petal blooms and then begin checking the size of the potatoes. Depending upon variety and weather conditions, potatoes may not bloom, so dig when the leaves on your potato vines begin turning yellow. Alternately, when potatoes have reached desired size, cut off stems and let potatoes cure in the soil for 2 weeks to toughen skins for winter storage.

Storage

Let harvested potatoes cure in the shade for one or two days. Exposure to the sun turns the potato skin green, creating a moderately poisonous substance called solanine. Peel off any green skin before cooking. Rub off the excess soil, but do not scrub or soak the potatoes.

Store potatoes in a cool, dark, humid location, such as a basement. Do not store them with onions (which hastens deterioration), apples or pears (which encourage sprouting).

Try these unusual but easy-to-grow potatoes (from top left): 'Red Pontiac', 'Green Mountain', 'Purple Peruvian' and 'Caribe' (center).

In the Kitchen

What can't be done with potatoes? You can boil them, bake them, add them to stews, fry them for chips, make fries, toss them with salad dressing. Russet potatoes cook to a texture best for baking. Red Pontiacs mash to feather-light consistency. Kennebecs boil up perfectly. Fingerlings are superb when steamed and served whole with butter, or even with a sesame oil/cilantro/ginger/garlic dressing. Try the 'Red Warba' for that American classic, french fries.

Winter Vegetable Puree

Peel and dice an equal amount of parsnips, carrots and yellow Yukon potatoes. Cook each vegetable separately in boiling salted water until easily pierced with a fork. Drain the three vegetables thoroughly in a colander and puree them together. Add a small portion of cream or sour cream and butter until you reach your desired consistency. Season to taste with salt and pepper.

Harvest main crop potatoes after the tops have turned yellow. Carefully use a digging fork, or collect them by hand, to avoid damaging the spuds.

RADISHES

Raphanus sativus

Whether in containers or in garden beds, keep radishes growing quickly, in rich soil with lots of water. Harvest when young, before they get woody.

Radishes are one of the most satisfying garden crops. They grow very quickly and easily. The long-rooted French radishes grow almost as fast as the round types. The French love to eat them on picnics, sliced and served on top of baguettes, thinly brushed with sweet butter. Look for purple radishes, called 'Easter Egg', and long, slim all-white types called 'Icicle.' There are also half-pink and half-white types.

The oldest known radishes in cultivation are the Asian radishes. They have long, white roots full of crisp, rich flavor; they weigh a pound or more. Best known as daikon radishes, the mild-tasting root can be pickled fiery sweet-hot, grated with ginger and a dash of soy sauce as a side to meats, or thinly cut in rounds for salads.

Least known are the aerial radishes which are grown for their seedpods. They are crisp, prickly and pungent eaten raw in salads or quickly stir-fried or sautéed.

Type
Annual.

Size
From 4 inches to 24 inches tall, depending upon variety.

Recommended Varieties
The globe radish 'Easter Egg' is most fun to grow, with the little round globes that pop up in many different colors. 'White Icicle' is a delicious, long, crunchy radish, quite elegant when paired with carrots for easy snacking. 'White Celestial' is a mild daikon, while 'Long Black Spanish', with its black exterior and white flesh, is quite striking.

When to Plant
Cool seasons: early spring, late summer to fall. Some types tolerate heat.

Light
Full sun or bright shade.

Soil
Loose, rich soil.

How to Grow
Work compost into the soil for good moisture retention and loose soil composition. Sow seeds directly in the ground as early in the spring as the ground can be worked, planting them ½ inch deep. Spread seeds over a planting bed or plant in rows.

Thin small globe types to 1 inch apart, long-rooted radishes to 4 to 6 inches apart. Space aerial radishes 12 inches apart. Keep radishes well watered and plant small batches of quick-growing types for a succession of harvest. Radishes will grow in containers.

Propagation
Allow some open-pollination varieties to go to seed. Pick pods of aerial types when they get old and begin to turn color and dry. Store in paper bags in a warm, dry place until husks are totally dry.

Some 200 varieties of radishes are available to home gardeners. Anyone can grow them!

Daikon Radishes

This recipe, although geared for the flavor of daikon, works equally well with other radishes. Serve them straight out of the canning jar or use them as a basis for a crunchy salsa. Coarsely chopped and mixed with scallions and chopped tomatoes, the salsa makes a delicious topping to grilled meats.

2 daikon radishes or other radishes to make about 1½ pounds
2 medium-size carrots
2¾ cups 5-percent white wine vinegar
1 cup water
2 tablespoons sugar

3 teaspoons finely chopped fresh ginger
8 cloves garlic, halved
4 small dried hot chiles, 3 to 5 inches long
4 bay leaves

Cut daikon or other radishes in portions to fit into pint jars. Quarter long radishes and then slice into thin sections. Leave 1 inch headroom. Combine wine vinegar, water, sugar, ginger, garlic, chiles and bay leaves in a medium-size non-reactive saucepan and bring to a boil.

Place the radishes and carrots into 4 sterilized pint-size jars. Pour the vinegar mixture into the jars, leaving a ½ inch headroom. Seal the jars and process for 10 minutes. (See pages 144-147 for further canning tips, and safety considerations.)

Makes 4 pints.

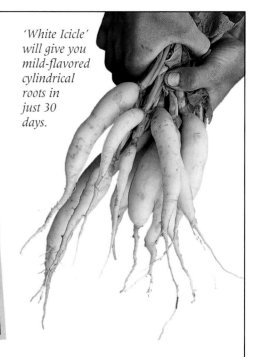

'White Icicle' will give you mild-flavored cylindrical roots in just 30 days.

Pests and Diseases

Radishes are susceptible to cabbage root maggots. Use a cloth tunnel barrier after seeding, harvest promptly, and rotate every season. Holes drilled in the roots indicate root maggots. If root maggots are a problem, cover seedlings with a floating row cover.

Daikon radishes are also known as Asian, Oriental or Japanese radishes. In the garden they usually take a little longer to grow, but yield large roots that store well.

Harvest

Twenty-four days for short season varieties, 50 to 75 days for daikon types. Harvest globe types when olive-sized, before the root becomes tough and fibrous and unpleasantly hot. Harvest longer growing types when they reach mature size as specified on the seed packages; this helps avoid damage from nematodes or root maggots.

Storage

Cut off tops from roots and store in plastic bags in the produce drawer of the refrigerator for 3 to 5 days. To refresh, wash and soak for 30 minutes in ice cold water.

In the Kitchen

Radishes' crisp texture has long added crunch to salads. Use raw radishes to make salsas, top sandwiches in place of lettuce, or pickle as an hors d'oeuvre. Add the long-rooted types to stews or sauté quickly as a side vegetable dish. Try stir-frying the daikon/long white radishes quickly in Asian recipes: use like water chestnuts, just warmed through to preserve the crunchy texture. Asian radishes can be pickled as

Red-fleshed radishes make zesty garnishes when grated or pickled.

the Korean kim chee or the Japanese takuan.

GARDEN FILLERS

Intercrop quick-growing radishes between lettuces, in pumpkin patches or elsewhere in the garden, to utilize a patch of ground that's temporarily bare. A month later, just when the longer-lived crop begins to stretch out, harvest the radishes.

RUTABAGAS AND TURNIPS

Brassica napus and *Brassica rapa*

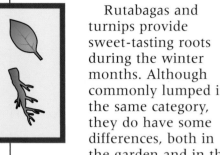

Rutabagas and turnips provide sweet-tasting roots during the winter months. Although commonly lumped in the same category, they do have some differences, both in the garden and in the kitchen.

The turnip was always an important food crop for European peasants before the discovery of the potato. And the savory green tops can be steamed or stir-fried as a green vegetable. Harvest turnips when they are the size of walnuts; eat both the root and the top at the same time.

Rutabagas, on the other hand, need to stay in the ground until they sweeten after several frosts.

Type
Biennials, grown as annuals.

Size
Depends upon the variety, from tiny 1 inch diameter turnips to big 1-pound rutabagas.

Recommended Varieties
For turnips, look for the gourmet hit 'Di Milan', or 'Hakurei'. The old standard white turnip with purple shoulders is 'Purple Top'. Try 'York' or 'Gilfeather' in rutabagas, where there is limited choice of varieties.

When to Plant
Early spring or mid-summer for a fall crop.

Light
Full sun.

Soil
Loose soil, well-worked with compost. Keep the soil pH about 6 to 7.

How to Grow
Sow seeds of turnips directly in the garden as early in the spring as the ground can be worked. Sow rutabagas after July 1. Work compost into the soil for good moisture retention

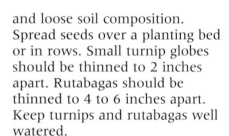

'Scarlet Ball' is a crisp turnip with white flesh.

and loose soil composition. Spread seeds over a planting bed or in rows. Small turnip globes should be thinned to 2 inches apart. Rutabagas should be thinned to 4 to 6 inches apart. Keep turnips and rutabagas well watered.

Propagation
Seed.

Pests and Diseases
Rutabagas and turnips are susceptible to cabbage root maggots. Use a cloth tunnel barrier after seeding and harvest

Don't forget to use the greens of turnips. They are packed with vitamins A, C and E, plus potassium and iron. If you harvest greens before pulling the root, leave at least 5 or 6 leaves on the root for more growth.

Rutabagas differ from turnips in their yellow flesh, longer growing season, and better keeping qualities. Some say that rutabagas are sweeter too.

Rutabagas don't need much preparation. Just scrub off the soil and then use them much as you would carrots.

Braised Young Turnips in Green Nests

16 small turnips (about walnut-sized) with tops
2 tablespoons peanut or canola oil
1 teaspoon finely chopped garlic
2 tablespoons sugar
¼ cup walnuts
Salt and pepper to taste

Separate the green turnip tops from the turnips. Wash thoroughly and set aside. In a medium-size sauté pan, add 1 tablespoon of the oil, the turnip tops and the garlic. Stir continually as if you were stir-frying, until the tops turn color and taste tender. Salt and pepper to taste and set aside.

Cut the turnips in half. In a medium-size sauté pan, add the other tablespoon of canola oil and heat to medium. Add the turnips and sauté for 4 to 5 minutes, stirring constantly. Turn the heat to low and add the sugar, continuing to stir the turnips. The sugar will begin to caramelize and turn brown. Add the walnuts. Continue to cook for an additional minute.

Divide the greens between 4 salad plates, making a nest of greens on each plate. Divide the turnip mixture between the four plates, spooning the mixture into the nest. Serve immediately.

Serves 4.

promptly. Rotate your planting location every season.

Harvest

Turnips—30 to 40 days; rutabagas—95 to 100-plus days.

Start harvesting turnips when they are 2 inches in diameter and finish before the root becomes tough and fibrous (about 3 inches).

Harvest rutabagas at about 4 inches in diameter. If you can, wait to harvest rutabagas until after several nights of frost sweeten the roots. In mild-winter areas, leave some crop under mulch and harvest through the winter as desired.

Storage

Cut off tops from turnips and store in plastic bags in the produce drawer of the refrigerator. Use turnip tops as quickly as possible. Store turnips for up to 5 days. Rutabagas can be stored in the refrigerator or in a cool dark place for months.

In the Kitchen

Young turnips don't need to be peeled, but mature turnips should be. Use turnips and rutabagas like carrots: baked, stewed and puréed. Use tops from young turnips (harvested when the globes are about 2 inches in diameter) like kale or collards.

Harvest rutabagas as soon as they're usable—2 or 3 inches across—but aficionados keep them in the ground until after at least one frost.

Harvest turnips when they're young—about an inch or two in diameter. Larger ones will take longer to cook.

SQUASH AND PUMPKINS

Cucurbita spp.

This *Cucurbita* family—which includes all the members of the gourd family from squash, pumpkins and cucumbers to bitter melon—has long fed humankind.

Archeological excavations in Central America and Mexico have uncovered remains of gourds, squash and pumpkins dated from 9000 B.C. Most of the *Cucurbita* came from the Americas, where their importance is well documented in stone-carved pictures of squash blossoms, and myths central to indigenous people in the Americas.

Although originally prized as household utensils and storage bowls, the hard-shelled varieties became cultivated for their nutritious seeds. With cross-breeding, the flesh was eventually valued as food.

Sorting out the different families is tricky because the terms "pumpkin" and "squash" do not relate to the actual varieties. Thinking of the squash family in terms of summer squash and winter squash clears the picture somewhat. Summer squash are the perishable, soft-skinned types. All pumpkins and squash with hard shells are winter squash.

Young zucchini served with the blossom still attached is an easy kitchen delicacy.

Summer Squash
Cucurbita pepo

You can always identify *Cucurbita pepo* by their five-sided stems and prickly spines. Although zucchini bears the brunt of many gardener jokes because of its abundant harvest, all the summer squash produce prolifically without much attention.

There are many different varieties of the summer squash, from the round scalloped pattypans to 'Zucchetta Rampicante', a long, snake-like variety with an intense and rich flavor. The Italian heirloom, 'Cucuzzi', can grow to the size of a baseball bat.

For households of four people, four bushes will provide enough squash—about 50 total pounds for 4 plants—for daily use. There is no reason to become inundated by your squash plants.

Paradoxically, the secret to keeping your summer squash under control is to continue picking them. Check under the leaves to find the baby squash which are exquisitely tender and sweet. Harvest the long types at about 3 inches in diameter and the round types when they are 2 inches in diameter.

Harvesting the squash blossoms, both the male and the female, also limits your harvest. Stuff blossoms with a cheese or meat filling, dip in an egg batter and sauté. Heirloom varieties of squash are quite healthy and seed saving is easy. But squash cross-pollinate easily, so to save seeds you must carefully follow seed-saving procedures (see page 20).

Type
Annual.

Size
About 3 to 4 feet tall and as wide, or bigger, depending upon variety.

Recommended Varieties

Growing summer squash becomes a chore only when the gardener plants too much of a good thing. Limit the total number of bushes but plant a variety. For zucchini, try 'Costana Romanesco' and 'Gold Rush', a

Squash comes in a dazzling number of types, including summer squash pattypan, yellow summer and zucchini; and winter types acorn, butternut and hubbard.

SAVING SQUASH SEED

If you want to save seed from non-hybrid varieties, learn to tell the difference between the female and the male squash blossoms. The flowers with a bump—the immature squash at the end of the bloom—are female blossoms. Those flowers with just a straight stem are the males.

To pollinate blossoms, tape shut the male blossom before it opens; try to do this the day before you think it would open. Tape together the petals of a female flower before it opens.

The next day, pick the male flower and strip off its petals. Gently open the petals of the female blossom and paint the stigma of the female with the anthers that hold the pollen from the male blossom. Tape up the petals of the female blossom to prevent any stray pollen from cross-pollinating the female blossom.

Save the squash from that blossom for seed, confident that it is pure and not cross-pollinated.

long golden zucchini. 'Zephyr' is a straight yellow crookneck with a green tip. Little yellow pattypans like 'Sunburst' or the green 'Peter Pan' go well together. 'Ronde de Nice' is a tasty, round zucchini imported from France. The vining 'Zucchetta Rampicante' delivers a meaty and delicious S-shaped fruit, quite unlike any other.

When to Plant
As soon as the soil warms and the night temperatures don't drop below 50°F.

Light
Full sun.

'Sundance' is a reliable yellow crookneck squash.

Soil
Rich, well-drained soil with plenty of well-rotted compost worked in at least 2 weeks before planting.

How to Grow
For hill planting, mound the soil in the prepared planting area to form a round bed that is 2 feet in diameter and about 6 inches higher than the normal soil level. Sow four seeds on each hill, pushing them down 1 inch deep. Pat the

The tenderest squashes are picked young, but larger ones are great on the grill or stuffed.

soil down firmly. Thin to the two strongest seedlings when plants are 3 inches high. Leave 5 feet between hills.

'Sunburst' is a delicious scallop or pattypan hybrid that won an All America Selections award.

Squash-Blossom Fritters

1 cup ricotta cheese
¼ cup grated Parmesan or hard Jack cheese
1 tablespoon flour
½ teaspoon fresh thyme
Salt and pepper to taste
12 squash blossoms
1 egg, beaten
Flour for coating
Peanut or canola oil for frying

In a medium bowl, mix together the ricotta cheese, grated cheese, flour and thyme. Season to taste with the salt and pepper. Divide the mixture among the squash blossoms, filling each of the blossoms.

Dunk each blossom in the egg, then coat the blossom lightly with flour. Add enough oil to a large sauté pan to cover the bottom ¼ inch deep. Heat the oil and brown the fritters. Drain the fritters on paper towels and serve immediately.

Serves 4.

Propagation

By seed or by transplants. The *Cucurbita* family cross-pollinates easily, So saving seeds must be done carefully. Hand-pollinate flowers (see page 125) and tie up blooms to prevent any additional pollination from wind or insects.

Pests and Diseases

Striped cucumber beetles will damage plants. Hand pick bugs.

Harvest

Pick summer squash when young, about 4 to 6 inches long. If round or scallop shaped, pick

Zucchini aren't just uniform dark green. They come in green stripes (shown here), and even gold (e.g. 'Gold Rush'). If you want a round zucchini, try 'Ronde de Nice'.

at 2 to 4 inches in diameter. Continued picking extends the harvest. If the harvest threatens to overwhelm you, begin picking the male and female squash flowers to stuff and fry in batter.

Storage

Summer squash do not store well. For the freshest, sweetest taste, use within one to two days of picking.

In the Kitchen

From pickles to quick sautées to pies, squash have a permanent place in the kitchen. If you miss a zucchini and it grows too large, stuff it for an entrée, slice it for pickles, grate it for cake or grind it up for soup.

Pumpkins and winter squash are really members of the same family, and grow under the same conditions.

Winter Squash,
Cucurbita spp.

Like pumpkins, some of the *Cucurbita* family develop such hard shells as they mature that they store exceedingly well. Some of the summer squash, if left, will develop a hard shell that preserves them; but when opened to eat, they lack the fine flesh of the winter squash.

Summer squash are eaten when small and tender, quickly cooked. Winter squash, with their hard shells, must be peeled or long-baked before using.

The Naragansett Indians called their *Cucurbita* "askutasquash." We celebrate Thanksgiving with pumpkin pies, a reminder that the colonists discovered pumpkins—a winter squash—through the generosity of the Native Americans.

Pumpkins have long been a useful winter staple, although now that we have refrigeration, they have been diminished merely to pie filling. Native Americans baked them whole in their fires, cut them open to eat seasoned with animal fat and honey.

American colonists soon adapted the recipe, opened the pumpkin and filled it with apples, raisins and spices, then baked it in the fire. By 1796, Amelia Simmons called for "pumpkin pie"

Acorn squashes are great keepers and require less time to mature (85 days or so) than most other winter squashes. Try 'Ebony Acorn', 'Table King', 'Jersey Golden Acorn' or 'Cream of the Crop'.

while other early settlers were making beer with pumpkin, persimmons and maple sugar.

Both Washington and Jefferson grew squash and pumpkins in their kitchen gardens. Ship captains, ever vigilant to find new kinds of food that would keep over long voyages, discovered additional varieties of squash in Central America. A squash brought to Marblehead by ship captain Knott Martin in 1842 was first raised by a Mrs. Hubbard. Thereafter it became ever known as Hubbard squash.

Winter squash 'Honey Delight'.

Type
Annual.

Size
Vines can grow 10 to 15 feet long. Smaller bush types still take up a 4 foot diameter.

Recommended Varieties
The colors and shapes of winter squash are so pleasing to the eye that you might want to grow one of each. But don't forget that the rambling vines take up a huge amount of garden space!

Try the delicious 'Delicata', a small, elongated type that makes fine eating. 'Red Kuri' has flesh so sugary that a puree will ferment when left out of the refrigerator overnight. 'Sweet Dumpling' is another small squash that has great flavor and also keeps well. 'Blue Hubbard' will give you a 20-pound wonder for plenty of soup. And, of course, spaghetti squash is a favorite for many children.

When to Plant
In spring, after the last chance of frost has passed and when the nights do not fall below 50°F, you can safely sow your winter squash outside. If you prefer, start the seeds indoors four to six weeks before the last frost.

Light
Full sun.

Soil
Prepare the soil properly, mixing in compost and well-rotted manure.

How to Grow
For hill planting, mound the soil in the prepared planting area to form a round bed that is 2 feet in diameter and about 6 inches higher than the normal soil level. Sow four seeds on each hill, pushing them down 1 inch deep. Pat the soil down firmly. Thin to the two strongest seedlings when plants are 3 inches high. Leave 10 feet in between hills.

Propagation
By seed or transplants.

Pests and Diseases
Squash bugs, cucumber beetles, and borers are the main pests. Use floating row covers for the first two. To discourage borers, cover the bottom of plants with 6 to 8 inches of soil. To prevent diseases, keep plants growing vigorously in fertile soil. Give plenty of water, but don't water the leaves.

Harvest
When your fingernail cannot easily pierce the skin. Leave 2 to 4 inches of stem on each squash.

Storage
Let winter squash dry on the vines, then gather them and store in a cool, 60°F location until they are needed. Any squash with nicks or breaks in the skin needs to be used right away.

In the Kitchen
Use winter squash in soups, soufflés, pies, custards, stews or mashed like sweet potatoes. Grilled or roasted squash is delicious.

Pumpkin 'Tallman'; winter squashes 'Waltham Butternut' and 'Ebony Acorn'.

Growing pumpkins is a wonderful way for kids to get into gardening.

To grow larger pumpkins, remove all but one or two fruiting blossoms from the vine.

Pumpkins
Curcurbita pepo or *Cucurbita maxima*, true French pumpkins

Make lots of room for pumpkins by interplanting them with corn, as the Native Americans have for centuries, or surround the hill with spring salad greens you will harvest before the pumpkins start to sprawl. Try growing beans, cucumbers and melons up on trellises with pumpkins spreading out as a groundcover.

As the pumpkins grow, set the young fruit on hay, cardboard or even wood to raise them off the ground and keep the skin off of the damp soil.

Type
Annual.

Size
Vines can grow 10 to 15 feet long.

Recommended Varieties
Bias plays a large part, but two pumpkins I simply wouldn't be without are 'Lumina', the white skinned pumpkin, and 'Rouge d'Etampes', the flattened disk-shaped pumpkin with a delicious meat.

When to Plant
In spring, after the last chance of frost has passed and when the nights do not fall below 50°F, you can safely sow your pumpkins outside. If you prefer, start the seeds indoors four to six weeks before the last frost.

Light
Full sun.

This pumpkin will be mature when the rind hardens and the vines yellow.

'LUMINA' PUMPKINS

Pumpkin has long been a descriptive term for the color orange, but creamy white 'Lumina' challenges the term. Recently, white pumpkins have masqueraded as ghostly, carved Halloween pumpkins but the flavor of 'Lumina's' flesh makes it a star in the kitchen as well. Actually, white pumpkins have been around for a long time. Giacomo Castelvetro describes white pumpkins in his 1614 book on Italian fruits, herbs and vegetables.

TIP   PUMPKIN POT

For an elegant occasion, bake one pumpkin, scrape out the meat and make into soup. Cut open the top of a second pumpkin, clean out the seeds, and warm the pumpkin in the oven just before you plan to serve the soup. Dish the hot soup into the warmed pumpkin as an elegant pumpkin container.

Yes, even pumpkins can be grown in containers. Use a whiskey barrel or large pot, and choose a miniature variety—'Baby Bear', 'Baby Boo', 'Jack Be Little' or 'Sweetie Pie'.

Soil

Prepare the soil properly, mixing in the all-purpose, slow-release fertilizer pellets according to the directions on the container.

How to Grow

For hill planting, mound the soil in the prepared planting area to form a round bed that is 2 feet in diameter and about 6 inches higher than the normal soil level. Sow four seeds on each hill, pushing them down 1 inch deep. Pat the soil down firmly. Thin to the two strongest seedlings when plants are 3 inches high. Leave 10 feet between hills.

Propagation

Seed or transplant seedlings.

Pests and Diseases

Squash bugs, cucumber beetles, and borers are the main pests. Use floating row covers for the first two. To discourage borers, cover the bottom of plants with 6 to 8 inches of soil. To prevent diseases, keep plants growing vigorously in fertile soil. Give plenty of water, but don't water the leaves.

Harvest

Harvest the pumpkins when your fingernail cannot easily pierce the skin, leaving 2 to 4 inches of stem on each pumpkin.

Storage

Let the pumpkins dry on the vines, then gather and store them at 60°F. Any pumpkin with nicks or breaks in the skin needs to be used right away.

In the Kitchen

Use pumpkins in soups, soufflés, pies, custards, stews or mashed like sweet potatoes. Grilled or roasted pumpkin is delicious.

Quick Pumpkin Loaf

This moist cake tastes even better if you have dried your own raisins. Use red flame grapes for great results. Dehydrate the grapes until they are just wrinkled and leathery, not hard; store in zip lock bags in the freezer until ready to use.

1 small pumpkin
2 cups unbleached all-purpose flour
2 teaspoons baking soda
½ teaspoon salt
1½ teaspoons cinnamon
1 cup sugar

½ cup peanut or canola oil
2 eggs, at room temperature
1½ cups cooked pumpkin
1 cup raisins
1 cup pecans, toasted

Preheat the oven to 350°F.

Cut the small pumpkin in half and clean out the seeds. A melon scooper works well. Turn the pumpkin halves upside down on a cookie sheet and place on the lower rack of the oven. Add as much water to the cookie sheet as possible. Bake for 1½ hours or until the pumpkin is soft. Scrape out 1½ cups of pumpkin meat and process in a blender or food processor until smooth.

In a large mixing bowl, combine the flour, baking soda, salt and cinnamon. In a medium mixing bowl, combine the sugar, oil, eggs and blended pumpkin. Beat the ingredients together thoroughly. Add the pumpkin mix to the dry ingredients, stirring just until the ingredients are moistened. Gently stir in the raisins and the pecans.

Pour the batter into a greased 9- x 5- x 3-inch loaf pan. Bake the loaf at 350°F for 40 to 50 minutes or until the edges pull away from the sides of the pan and a toothpick inserted in the center comes out clean.

TOMATOES

Lycopersicon lycopersicum or *esculentum*

Some historians claim that Thomas Jefferson was the first to grow tomatoes in the United States. Others allege that tomatoes were already widely grown throughout the southern colonies, imported by the Spanish missionary fathers who brought them from Central and South America. Regardless of this historical bickering, the tomato was one of the new American fruits discovered during the Spanish conquest of Central America in the 1500s.

After 400 years of breeding, there are colors, shapes and tastes for every palette, which make the smooth, round, dull-colored tomato imitations in grocery stores seem dull and uninspiring.

When choosing your varieties, vary your harvest by selecting types of the thin-sided, slicing tomatoes for salads and fresh use—like 'Early Girl' and 'Dona'—and the thick-walled varieties best for cooking such as 'Roma'.

Tomatoes grow in two different patterns. The indeterminate varieties grow, flower and produce fruit over a long growing season. The determinates only grow to a certain size and produce, bloom and fruit for a limited time.

To upset this tidy distinction, growers have developed a new type called "husky" with limited growth and a longer growing season. These seeds can be found in catalogs, sometimes under the label of "dwarf indeterminate."

If you have lots of room, the indeterminate varieties produce buckets of juicy, delicious tomatoes. For best results, they need to be staked or contained in wire

Fresh tomatoes from the garden. It's no wonder that tomatoes are America's favorite garden vegetable.

A dazzling palette of delicious tomatoes.

'Floramerica' is an All America Selections winner. It gives 6- to 8-ounce fruits.

cages or even tied to rows of stakes like grapevines. The determinate varieties will grow in containers easily, but be sure to establish a consistent watering pattern for best fruiting results.

'Sungold' puts out a heavy crop of inch-wide fruits on indeterminate vines.

Start your own seedlings to grow the most interesting varieties. And check with local nurseries to see what they have ordered; request they reserve some unusual varieties for you. If you do not want to grow your own, check with your neighbors or other gardeners for a swap of seeds for seedlings.

Type
Perennial, grown as an annual.

Size
Dwarf types can be a 3-foot-high bush suitable for a container. Indeterminate cherry varieties grow up 8 to 10 feet tall and 6 feet wide.

Recommended Varieties
Of the cherry tomatoes, 'Early Cascade' comes on quickly and stays productive. 'Green Grape', although slightly bigger, is quite delicious and is harvested when green in color. 'Sungold', with its spicy taste, is a must. Although 'Early Girl' remains a reliable favorite, the harder to find 'Dona' has a better taste and texture. See the list below for more choices.

When to Plant
In spring, after the last chance of frost has passed and when the nights do not fall below 50°F. It's a good idea to start the

HEIRLOOM TOMATOES

Some of the more interesting varieties of tomatoes now available in seeds are called "old-fashioned" or heirloom varieties. They are fun to grow, and some have corrugated shapes or blotches of special color. Many also pack a wallop of flavor for the kitchen, so if you have room, make a place for them. Try 'Costaluto Genovese', 'Mortgage Lifter' and 'Brandywine': types long swapped over the back fence they are so beloved. Save their seeds and pass them along to your friends and neighbors.

seeds indoors four to six weeks before the last frost.

Light
Full sun, although cherry tomatoes can take a bit of morning or afternoon shade.

Soil
Nitrogen-rich soil encourages tomatoes to grow leaves, not blooms. Tomatoes require quantities of potassium and phos-

'Roma VF' is a standby Italian plum tomato. It is a determinate plant.

NINE TOMATO TYPES YOU OUGHT TO TRY

'Big Beef' VFFNTA Hybrid: A brand new tomato and winner of the All America Selections Award. Touted for flavor and yield.

'Celebrity': A reliable determinate with flavor and yields.

'Costaluto Genovese': An heirloom with real old-fashioned flavor if in small production.

'Dona': Fabulous taste and texture in a tomato earlier than 'Early Girl'. Very prolific over a long season.

'Green Grape': Grape-sized and green when ripe.

'Husky Gold': One of the new dwarf indeterminates. Great for containers.

'Odoriko': A pink slicing tomato with delicious flavor.

'Sun Gold': A snappy-sweet cherry in an attractive gold color.

'Yellow Stuffer': A paste type that looks like a bell pepper. Great for stuffing, also good for drying.

Tomato Paste

Use cooking tomato varieties such as 'Roma' to make an intensely flavored tomato paste.

Cut tomatoes in half and place cut-side down on a baking sheet. Salt lightly. Place the tomatoes in a 300°F oven for 2 to 3 hours or until the tops of the tomatoes are brown and most of the juice has dried on the tray. Use a food strainer or food mill to separate out skins and seeds from the pulp. The resulting pulp mixture should be thick and sweet. If it seems too thin, pour it back onto the cookie sheet and continue to cook until it reaches the desired consistency. Pour into plastic freezer bags or containers and freeze. Or, if you choose, freeze the paste in ice cube trays. When frozen solid, store the blocks in plastic freezer bags. Each cube is approximately 2 tablespoons. When you have defrosted the paste for use, season to taste with garlic, herbs, salt and pepper.

phorus with only medium amounts of nitrogen. Work in quantities of well-rotted compost to combat disease microorganisms

in the soil. Heirloom varieties are susceptible to these diseases.

How to Grow

Make a wire cage for each plant; the circle of wire should have 6-inch openings, and be 24 inches in diameter and at least 4 feet high. You can also tie the plants to stakes, using cotton cloth strips loosely tied to stakes, to hold up the plant.

Early in the season when the plant has just started flowering, shake tomato cages daily to increase fruit set from increased pollen distribution. Work lots of organic compost into your planting beds and rotate your plants from year to year as a precautionary step: Tomatoes are prone to soil-borne diseases.

Tomatillos put out lots of fruit. If you let any mature ones drop without picking them up, you can bet you'll have volunteer plants next year.

TIP EXTENDING THE HARVEST

Just before the first frost, pull up tomato vines by the roots and hang them upside down in a cool, dark place. Your tomatoes will ripen gradually on the vine over several weeks. They do not taste as sweet as sun-ripened, but still are fresh and delicious.

'Sweet 100' is a cherry tomato that's easily grown in containers if you give it a little pruning.

Harvest tomatillos when the fruits swell, turn color and the husks break open.

tobacco mosaic virus (T) and alternaria (A). If you have good success with these tomatoes, try the less disease-resistant heirloom tomatoes.

Chewed leaves indicate the presence of the tomato hornworm, a large caterpillar that is so well camouflaged you may have difficulty seeing it. Pick them off by hand and discard.

Harvest

Pick tomatoes that are fully colored and plump. Determinate-growth tomatoes will set all their fruit at about the same time. Keep tomatoes picked to stimulate further production on indeterminate vines.

Storage

Do not refrigerate tomatoes; the chill turns the sugars into starch, destroying the tomato's flavor.

In the Kitchen

Paste varieties have been developed to have dense, thick-walled sides that, when cooked, melt into a rich sauce that clings to pasta and sings with

flavor. These types are often egg-shaped, and there are both determinate and indeterminate varieties available.

Juice or slicing varieties are best for eating fresh, because cooking them down only produces a watery sauce with little texture.

If you want to dry your own tomatoes, experiment with both varieties, because the slicing varieties will have a sweeter flavor but less bulk than the paste types. Dry cherry tomatoes for use all winter long.

Other Uses

Husk cherries (*Solanum melanocerasum*) and tomatillos (*Physalis ixocarpa*) are easily-grown relatives. Husk cherries can be used for jams and pies, while tomatillos star in Mexican salsas and sauces.

Most tomatoes need support. This method provides it and gives some protection from squirrels and other varmints.

Propagation

Seed and transplants. The side shoots of branches, known as suckers, can be rooted to make extra plants. Save the seeds of open-pollinated types.

Pests and Diseases

Grow plants that have been bred to resist verticillium wilt (V), fusarium wilt (F), nematodes (N),

CONTINUOUS HARVEST

Early-, mid- and late-season varieties relate to a specific number of days to flower and bear fruit. In nurseries, the tag may only give the number of days to fruit, so remember that early season tomatoes take 50 to 65 days from transplanting to harvest, midseason ones need about 65 to 80 days and late season plants 80 to 90 days or more. To have an extra-long harvest of tomatoes in your plot, try growing some of all three so you will be able to pick some varieties early and still have the pleasure of sampling the mid- and late-season varieties until the first frosts.

◆ CHAPTER 4 ◆

PRESERVING & PREPARING THE GARDEN'S BOUNTY

S ummer is at its harvest zenith with bushes laden with tomatoes, zucchini peaking out from underneath huge leaves, and pumpkins snaking around the garden. Neighbors shake their heads at generous offerings of summer squash and bushels of tomatoes. There's more in the garden than a household can eat, and if you stop picking, then the plants stop producing. What to do?

Before refrigeration, everyone had to preserve their harvest. You too can relish a pantry filled with homegrown harvest— whether frozen, canned, pickled or dried. It's easier facing the garden's shriveling stalks and vines when you have beans in the freezer, jars of pickles in the pantry and dried tomatoes all bagged up and ready to go.

We'll help you master all these preservation techniques.

And, whether you are preparing your harvest or eating it fresh, there are many strategies and techniques to preparing it great. We'll show you the secrets and provide valuable insights, right here.

DRYING VEGETABLES

In dried form, the year's harvest can feed you throughout the winter.

The first method of preserving food was drying. Our ancestors used the sun's heat to do the work of taking out moisture, so drying is a simple process. For those with limited freezer or storage space, drying is a good alternative to canning or freezing.

Dried vegetables have an intense flavor. Some, like beans and peas, need to be reconstituted in water before using. Others, like dried onions or herbs, can be added directly to a dish.

Drying Methods

Drying requires heat and air circulation in order to evaporate moisture from vegetables.

The most basic vegetable dryer is a large window screen placed on blocks above the ground where it receives full sun.

An electric dryer—either with a fan or without—is an investment that pays off in packages of dried vegetables and herbs. You can also dry vegetables in ovens, as long as you can set the oven temperature very low—about 145°F. Gas ovens warmed with a pilot light work equally well, but in both cases, use a thermometer to monitor the temperature. Crack open the oven door to keep air circulating.

Drying Chinese bitter melon.

Rotate the trays during the drying times, because heat patterns in dehydrators and ovens vary, drying some vegetables before the others. Check vegetables every half hour or so, as they can scorch.

How to Dry Vegetables

Wash vegetables clean with cold water. Do not soak them: vitamins easily leach out and the vegetables will take on more water, which increases drying time.

If you plan on long term storage (more than six months) for your dried vegetables, blanch

A dehydrator will pay for itself in a short time by giving you preserved vegetables and fruits that are both vitamin-rich and flavorful.

THE DOS AND DON'TS OF PRESERVING

- Always use the freshest, unblemished produce from the garden.
- Discard any bruised or damaged vegetables.
- Wash all vegetables, scrubbing with a brush if necessary to clean off dirt.
- Drain as dry as possible in a colander or on clean towels.
- Cut into uniform pieces.
- Follow recipes with utmost attention to quantities of salt, sugar or vinegar.
- When canning, time the steaming or water bath carefully according to the recipe's directions.

The delicious flavors and textures of preserved foods diminish over time. For the best results, use your products within six months to a year from the time you made them. Labeling the containers helps track their age. Should older products need to be discarded, you can always recycle them on the compost heap.

You can dry herbs in a microwave oven. Check the batch after each 30-second interval to avoid overcooking.

the vegetables first to stop the enzyme action that causes deterioration. Check individual blanching times for each vegetable (see chart on page 141).

Use a slicer or food processor to cut your vegetables uniformly so they dry at approximately the same time.

Judging when your products are dry and ready to store takes some experience. Vegetables are ready when they are pliable but dry and leathery on the outside. Rock-hard chips of tomatoes indicate too much exposure. Beans, peas and corn are ready when they do not give when squeezed. Check the trays once or twice daily, rotate them and remove pieces as they dry

Some experts recommend that you pasteurize all dried vegetables by placing a single layer on a cookie sheet in the oven at 175°F for 15 minutes. Most gardeners find their products keep satisfactorily without this step. Occasionally, a stored piece will develop mold. If so, discard it. When this happens, pasteurize the rest of the container's contents.

Storage

If you have space, you can store your dried vegetables in the freezer to keep them safe from rodents and bugs. Otherwise, store dried vegetables in a cool, dark space, and check your supplies regularly. Some cooks love the look and convenience of hanging drying ristras (chile strings), as well as garlic and onion braids, in the kitchen and near the stove. Although decorative, the exposure to warmth and light will actually cause them to lose their nutritional value faster, and they will spoil sooner.

Refreshing Dried Vegetables

Don't expect your dried vegetables to taste exactly like fresh. Use them in ways that enhance their concentrated flavors. Try them in soups and stews, pulverize them in a blender for a powder to add to salad dressings, soups, sauces and sandwiches.

To rehydrate or "refresh" your dried vegetables, soak them in cold water. Although vegetables take more time to rehydrate in cold water, they are more tender than when rehydrated in boiling water. Once plumped, rehydrated vegetables cook quickly.

Vegetables You Can Dry

Here are some examples of vegetables you can dry. A number of books are primers in drying and storing vegetables. Check Sources for some of these, page 154.

Beans

Some beans simply seem to hide under the leaves, and when you discover them, they are more seed than tender, succulent bean.

Pick these pods with large seeds and loosely string them together with a needle and heavy thread. Let your bean stringer

Dried beans are a staple of almost all cuisines. Keep yours in airtight jars.

Chili Powder

Make your own chili powder, either fiery hot or mild. Because it is homemade, the powder will be hotter and more flavorful than the purchased varieties. This creation combines the heat of the chiles with the flavor of herbs. Wash your hands carefully after preparing the chiles.

20 dried jalapeño chiles, about 1 ounce, tops cut off and the seeds tipped out (for hotter powder, cut off tops but leave seeds in)
1 teaspoon coriander seeds
½ teaspoon cumin seeds
½ teaspoon dried oregano

Toast the chiles, coriander and cumin seeds in a dry skillet, shaking constantly or on a roasting pan in the oven just until you smell a slight fragrance of chiles. Do not over-roast and burn the chiles or the seeds—this makes them bitter. They will continue to cook after they are taken off the heat.

In a coffee grinder used for spices or in a blender, grind together all the ingredients until they become grainy. You will not need a fine powder. Do not inhale the dust when you take off the lid.

Store in a glass container in a cool dark place. Use to taste in recipes. Beware: this powder is stronger and more flavorful than commercial chili powders.

Shelling dried beans.

dry in a warm, shady place until the beans turn a light brown color and begin to split open. Shell the beans and store them in a tightly stoppered glass jar in a cool, dark place. Some preservers like to put their beans in the freezer for several days to kill the little bean beetles which can destroy the beans.

You can also make what was historically called "leather britches" from your pole beans. Pick mature beans and lace them together with a sturdy thread and a large needle. Hang the strings of beans up in a warm dark place to dry thoroughly. When dry, store them in a plastic bags. To use, add the whole beans to stews and other long cooked dishes.

Corn

Pull back the husks, discard the silk, and tie in long chains

Homemade microwave popcorn.

by tying the husks together. Don't clump the ears too closely; air needs to circulate. Grind the dried kernels in a flour grinder, blender or food processor for a coarse cornmeal or soften the kernels by soaking in hot water until rehydrated for corn chowders and mixed vegetable soups.

Ristras (Chile Strings)

Dry your hot chiles that have developed to ripeness and keep them all winter long.

Pick peppers when they are fully ripe and bright red. String them together with a needle and strong thread. For aesthetics, you can separate the chiles with bay leaves. Hang your ristra to dry in a warm place out of direct sun. When the chiles have dried, leave them whole to toss into a stew or grind them up for chili powder, including the seeds if you like it *muy picante* (very hot).

To bring up the fullest flavor in a chile pepper before you use it, toast it in a warm, 300°F oven for 3 to 5 minutes, or until it gives off a fragrant odor. Do not burn chiles lest they become bitter.

Drying ears of corn for grinding.

Stringing dried chiles for ristras.

Tomatoes

Slice cherry or plum tomatoes in half, full-size tomatoes in ³⁄₈-inch slices. Slice them from the stem to the bottom, not horizontally. Salt lightly on both sides, then place in a dehydrator or on a screen so that air can circulate on both sides of the tomato.

Place the sheet in full sun or use a dehydrator. If drying outside in the sun, cover the tomatoes loosely with plastic wrap; leave the ends open to allow evaporation, and keep bugs and dust off. Do not overcrowd, to allow the tomatoes dry quickly without molding. When the tomatoes have thoroughly dried so that they are pliable but not moist, store them in glass containers or plastic sacks in a cool, dark place.

Drying pear tomato slices in the sun. Give them plenty of air circulation.

If you dry herbs on the stem, the leaves will come off easily.

Fines Herbes

This is a classic French herb blend to use in sauces, on salads and in salad dressing. Make it even if you are missing an ingredient. Simply experiment with substitutes, as would any French home chef. You can use the mixture in omelettes, salad dressings or stews.

3 parts dried chervil
2 parts dried parsley
1 part dried tarragon

½ part dried chives
½ part dried basil

Combine the herbs in a glass jar. Store the mixture in a cool dark place. Use according to your taste.

Herbs

The microwave dries herbs quickly and easily without loss of color.

Strip the leaves off the stems and place in the microwave on top of paper toweling. Do not overcrowd the leaves. Microwave for a minute at a time, checking closely to determine when the leaves are thoroughly dried and brittle. Overcooking the herbs may cause them to catch fire in the microwave.

Place the dried leaves in tightly covered glass containers and store them in a closed cupboard.

For capturing the fullest cooking flavor, don't crush the dried herbs until just before you use them. Discard the herbs after six months.

To grind the herbs, use a scrupulously clean coffee grinder or a blender. If you can, dedicate a grinder for herbs only. If you must share duties with coffee beans, after cleaning it you should grind up several pieces of bread to absorb any coffee oils left in the blender.

Flowers

Pick flowers just starting to bloom early in the morning. Hang them upside down in a warm, dark room away from direct sun. When the petals are stiff and brittle, pluck them off and store them in airtight jars.

To use, sprinkle over foods or pulverize in a clean spice blender. Dust the powder over cakes or on top of cream soups.

When drying rose petals, cut out the bitter tasting white triangle at the base of the leaf. Dry the leaves and store whole in a cool, dark place.

 TIP DRYING HERBS

Harvest herbs just before they blossom, when the aromatic oil content is the highest. If you are drying in bunches, hang by the stems so the oil will be concentrated in the tips of the leaves. Let the herbs dry in a warm, dark location. If the area is dusty, place the herb bunch inside a brown bag, close the bag and hang in a warm, dark area.

Tie and hang small clusters of herbs in a dark, airy place to dry them for storage.

Herbs de Provence

Another classic mix. Vary it according to your own personal taste.

1 part each: dried chervil, chives, parsley, lavender flowers and tarragon

Mix the herbs together. Store in a glass container in a cool, dark place.

Bouquet Garni

You can sprinkle this mild, all-purpose seasoning on top of stews, or add to baked goods or sandwiches. Larousse Gastronomique—one of the first encyclopedias of food, still full of useful information today—says the bouquet can include basil, celery, chervil, tarragon, burnet, rosemary and savory. Try different combinations depending on what you are serving. You can also tie fresh herbs together in a bundle, but in this case, increase the quantities of herbs, as the fresh herbs do not provide as intense a flavor as dried.

2 tablespoons dried celery chips
2 tablespoons each dried basil, oregano, parsley, thyme
2 bay leaves, center ribs removed and crumbled
1 tablespoon freshly ground pepper

Using a small, clean coffee grinder or a blender, grind the dried celery chips until they are ground into small pieces, about 20 to 30 seconds. Add the herbs and pepper to the container and blend for 10 seconds, just enough to crumble the leaves and mix everything. Store in a glass container in a cool, dark place.

Herbal Teas from Fresh or Dried Herbs

Inhale the fragrance arising from garden-fresh or dried herbs steeping in hot water and you will be instantly attracted to tisanes (*tee-zanes*). The clean, fresh taste of these herbal teas, with their pleasingly pale tints, have won over a demanding crowd of coffee gulpers newly sensitive to caffeine health issues and looking for gentler alternatives.

Herbal teas are humankind's oldest brewed pharmaceuticals, and anthropologists trek to jungles, high plateaus and deserts seeking shamans to teach them the curative properties of herbs.

In early America, colonists were tutored by native Americans on the culinary and medicinal purposes of local plants.

Stroll out to your garden to harvest the fresh aromatic leaves while the tea kettle comes to a boil on the stove. The fresh leaves release essential oils when infused in the boiling water. Don't expect the big bang of commercially packaged herbals with your own home-brewed; those trendy dried-leaf teas use additions of natural and/or artificial flavors to turn up the taste.

Save any leftover tea in the refrigerator. Use when you want a refreshing cold drink.

Sugar or a sweetener rounds out the flavors of tisanes, just as salt highlights savory tastes. Try a small amount of sweetener in the beginning to see what satisfies you. Use orange blossom honey with citrus flower teas, or sugar stored with cinnamon sticks or vanilla beans to add yet another subtle layer of flavor. Combine your infusions with white grape juice or apple juice if you wish to leave out the sugar.

For variety, some tea drinkers add dried chips of citrus peel, rose hips, sticks of cinnamon, dried apple nuggets, disks of ginger, lemon grass, clove or allspice. Part of the delight of making your own teas is the custom blending process, and making a tea of the moment to match your mood.

DRYING CITRUS PEELS

During winter months when citrus is at its best, start the habit of drying the peels of tangerines, tangelos or 'Minneola' oranges. Use a potato peeler or a knife to cut the bright orange peel away from the bitter white pith. Let the colored peel dry in a sunny windowsill or in a dehydrator until dry but still flexible. Store the dried peels in a glass jar in a cool dark place. The peels improve with age, so store a large quantity in order to have enough to last for several years. Add peels to herb blends, tomato-based stews or bean dishes.

Air-drying citrus peels will give you a supply of zesty rinds for a long time.

TIP YOUR OWN TEABAGS

Nichols Nursery (see Sources) offers individual paper tea bags which you fill and seal with an iron. You can easily make up your own sealed herb bags to drop into stews or sauces.

HOW TO MAKE TISANES (HERBAL INFUSIONS)

Bring a kettle of water to a full, rolling boil. Add a small amount of the hot water in a teapot and swirl to warm the pot thoroughly. Pour out the water and put in a generous amount of the leaves or flowers of the herbs. Add boiling hot water to the teapot and let the herbs infuse for at least 5 minutes to avoid a watery tea. Serve with pots of honey or sugar, and lemon or lime slices. Remember to:

- **Use a clean teapot;** tisanes absorb flavors of coffee or strongly-scented teas.

- **Pour boiling water over the herbs** to fully extract the flavors.

- **Steep for at least five minutes** to allow a richly flavored tea. Keep hot water on hand in case you need to dilute the tea.

- **Serve the tea in your most translucent china cups** or small juice glasses so the colors can be appreciated. Add a single leaf or blossom to each cup if you wish.

SOME TEA COMBINATIONS

- Lemon thyme and peppermint
- Lemon balm and chamomile
- Lemon verbena with a dash of rosemary
- Sage, lemon thyme and mint
- Pineapple sage and lemon blossoms
- Sage, lemon balm and hyssop
- Orange blossom and lavender
- Anise hyssop and lemon thyme
- Lemon verbena and rose petals (from heavily scented varieties; remove bitter white heel at the base)

Vegetable Spice

This is another multipurpose spice. Sprinkle it on top of pasta, season bagels and cream cheese, add it to soups to deepen their flavor. Without the salt, it becomes a tasty salt substitute. Experiment with proportions and mixtures to tailor blends to your satisfaction.

¼ cup dried celery
¼ cup dried carrots
¼ cup dried peppers
¼ cup dried mushrooms
2 tablespoons dried cherry tomatoes
1 teaspoon chile pepper seeds, optional

2 tablespoons dried parsley
1 tablespoon dried thyme
2 bay leaves, center ribs removed and crumbled
1 tablespoon kosher salt

In the container jar of a blender, combine the celery, carrots, peppers, mushrooms and tomatoes. Process until the pieces are finely chopped. Add the parsley, thyme and bay leaf. Process briefly to stir, about 10 seconds or until the texture is that of coarse powder. Add the tablespoon of salt to the vegetable blend, mix and pour into a glass container. Store the container in a cool, dark place.

Note: It is easiest to blend ingredients when they are freshly dried and crisp. If the vegetables have not been kept in airtight containers, they will be difficult to break down in small pieces.

VEGETABLE BLANCHING CHART

A quick blanching stops enzyme action, something you may want to do before drying or freezing vegetables. For the best results, remember to choose vegetables about the same size in each batch you are blanching. Times are given in a range to account for the differing sizes from small to large. Before processing your entire batch, run a test trial with just a few to make sure you do not overcook the vegetables.

Artichoke: Peel off outer leaves. Cut off bottom stem and trim top. Steam blanch 8 to 10 minutes.

Asparagus: Sort for size and trim stems. Steam blanch 2 to 4 minutes.

Beans, lima: Shell beans. Steam blanch 2 to 4 minutes.

Beans, shell, green: Shell beans. Steam blanch 1½ minutes.

Beans, snap, green, or yellow: Harvest beans when small, sort for size and trim stems. Steam blanch 3 to 4 minutes.

Beets: Trim off tops and cook beets until tender. Skin beets, slice into uniform pieces and pack.

Broccoli: Cut heads into uniform pieces. Steam blanch 3 to 5 minutes.

Brussels sprouts: Peel off outer leaves. Steam blanch 3 to 5 minutes.

Cabbage or Chinese cabbage: Peel off outer leaves. Cut into wedges. Steam blanch 5 minutes.

Carrots: Trim off tops and bottom roots. Cut into uniform pieces. Steam blanch 4 to 5 minutes.

Cauliflower: Cut heads into uniform pieces. Steam blanch 3 to 5 minutes.

Celery: Separate stalks. Trim off leaves and cut stalks into 2-inch long pieces. Steam blanch 3 to 5 minutes. Freeze leaves separately for use as seasoning in soups and stews.

Corn, whole kernel: Steam blanch 6 to 8 minutes. Cut off kernels and freeze.

Corn, on-the-cob: Cut into pieces to fit the freezing container. Steam blanch 6 to 8 minutes.

Greens, beets, chard, collards, kale, mustard, spinach: Use only leaves. Steam blanch 3 minutes.

Okra: Trim stems. Steam blanch 5 minutes.

Parsnips: Trim off tops and bottom roots and sort for size. Steam blanch 4 to 5 minutes.

Peas, green: Harvest peas when small. Shell. Steam blanch 1½ minutes.

Peppers, hot or sweet: No blanching necessary. Slice, seed and pack.

Pumpkin or winter squash: Cut in half, seed, and bake in a 350°F oven until tender. Spoon out meat, mash and pack.

Rutabagas: Trim off tops and bottom roots. Slice or dice. Steam blanch 3 minutes.

Summer squash: Harvest squash when small. Trim top and slice. Steam blanch 1 minute.

Tomatoes: No blanching necessary. Pack whole, unpeeled tomatoes into containers.

Turnips: Trim off tops and cook turnips until tender. Skin, slice into uniform pieces and pack.

FREEZING FOOD

Corn and tomatoes, ready for the freezer.

Vegetables frozen fresh from the garden have good flavor, color and texture. The amount of space you have in your freezer section is the only limiting factor to your harvest. Jars take up more room than plastic freezer bags. Check your freezer regularly so you can use up all your supplies by the time the spring garden begins to produce again. Flavor and texture in frozen vegetables diminish after 4 to 6 months.

How to Freeze Vegetables

Even after vegetables are picked, the enzymes that cause them to ripen continue to work, speeding them to decay. A quick blanching of most vegetables before you freeze them destroys the enzymes, preserving the flavor and texture of vegetables.

When blanching, you are not cooking the vegetables you are just warming them through enough to destroy the enzymes. Tomatoes and peppers are two vegetables which do not need blanching before freezing.

First, wash all vegetables before cutting them into equal-sized pieces. Use a slicer or food processor to cut your vegetables uniformly so they freeze at approximately the same time.

Frozen Fruit Blocks

This process works for all varieties of fruit but melons are exquisite.

Peel and seed melons. Whirl the fruit either individually or in combinations in a food processor or blender. Add sugar and lemon juice to taste. Pour the fruit mixture into ice cube trays. When frozen solid, remove the blocks and store in freezer bags. To use, let the blocks defrost slightly then add them to a blender with fruit juice, milk or ice cream for instant fruit smoothies.

TIP   FOOD BANK CONTRIBUTIONS

If your garden harvest gets way out of hand, and you really can't keep up with it, call your local food bank or food kitchen to make a contribution. Fresh produce is often difficult for them to procure and they will be very grateful for your donation. Garden-fresh vegetables should never go to waste.

Frozen Herb Blocks

Strip the leaves off 2 cups each fresh basil and parsley and blanch them in boiling water for 30 seconds. The blanching keeps the basil leaves from turning black. Blend the herbs together in a blender or food processor with enough olive oil to make a loose paste.

Fill an ice cube tray with the herb mixture to make individual herb blocks. When frozen solid, store the blocks in plastic freezer bags. Each cube is approximately 2 tablespoons' worth of that herb.

Toss a block into soups, sauces or stews to add a flash of summer herbal essence. Mix different combinations of herbs to discover the blends you prefer. Try tarragon and parsley, or rosemary, thyme and parsley.

To transform this herb mixture into pesto, defrost the number of blocks you need for a pesto sauce recipe. Add garlic, pine nuts and Parmesan cheese in correct proportions according to your recipe and blend in a food processor.

Preparing sweet pepper slices for freezing.

To blanch, boil water in a large pot. When the water is boiling, lower the prepared vegetables in a strainer until they are totally immersed and cover the pot. Blanching times vary for different vegetables (see chart, page 141).

When the blanching time is up, remove the vegetables, drain and quickly immerse them in a large bath of ice water. Add more ice if the water warms up; you want to stop the vegetables from cooking as quickly as possible.

Remove the vegetables from the water as soon as they feel cool to the touch. Do not let the vegetables soak. Drain the vegetables thoroughly, pack them into your containers and freeze as soon as possible.

Containers

Containers must be moisture- and vapor-proof to prevent evaporation and preserve the best quality of the vegetables. Glass, rigid plastic and metal containers are vapor-proof. Plastic bags are vapor-resistant so they are not the best for long-term storage. But if you are planning to use your vegetables within 3 to 6 months, the plastic freezer bags work fine. Light plastic bags or paper cartons do not make satisfactory containers.

Choose containers in serving sizes appropriate for your household so that when you defrost your vegetables, you use them up within a day.

Packing and Storing

Chill the food well before you pack your bags, so the contents freeze as quickly as possible. This helps maintain the food's color, texture and flavor.

Pack the food as tightly as possible in the container and try to get out as much air out as you can. When you are using plastic bags, seal them almost totally closed, insert a straw, and suck out the last of the air. Quickly withdraw the straw and seal the package so the contents are as much vacuum sealed as you can manage without a machine.

You do not need to use canning jars when freezing. Any glass jar will do. However, make sure all jars are clean and sterilized. Wipe the tops before you screw on the lids for the best possible seal. Don't forget to label the contents and the date.

A frozen vegetable mix that will make a warming winter soup many months after the harvest.

Frozen Tomatoes

If you get behind in your processing of tomatoes, wash, dry and toss them into the freezer without any preparation. When they have frozen solid, store them in plastic freezer bags. As the tomatoes defrost, peel off the skins and discard. Cut tomatoes in half and squeeze out seeds. Add the tomatoes to winter stews and soups.

CANNING

Any good canning guide will give you the proper processing times and procedures for individual vegetables and fruits.

Too many peppers and tomatoes? You can can 'em.

Canning protects food by heating a sealed jar to a temperature that destroys harmful organisms such as molds, yeast and bacteria. As the jar is sealed there can be no further contamination. Fruits, which are high in acid and sweet with sugar, are usually canned in a sugar syrup and consequently have a lower concentration of potentially harmful organisms.

Vegetables, with the exception of tomatoes, are low in acid, and without proper preparation, are more vulnerable to contamination, You must process low-acid vegetables in a pressure canner at a higher heat, up to 250°F, in order to destroy these contaminants.

Clostridium botulinum causes botulism, which in severe cases can be deadly. However, there are many recipes which preserve vegetables safely without a pressure canner. None of the recipes in this section call for the use of a pressure canner, and they all contain enough vinegar and/or sugar to be processed safely at home.

High-acid vegetables like tomatoes can be safely canned in a steam or water bath kettle. High-acid foods need lower temperatures to destroy organisms because fewer pests are able to exist in the highly acidic environment. Low-acid vegetables pickled in five percent vinegar solutions and salt are also protected.

There are two kinds of canners for low-temperature canning. The water bath covers jars with boiling water to raise the temperature of the contents. The steam canner surrounds jars with steam. Both are highly effective in destroying any contaminants when you follow directions and time the canning process accurately.

A little time spent canning your harvest will give you months and months of tasty rewards.

Preserved vegetables from last season's harvest are beautiful, flavorful and delicious.

DANGER—SIGNS OF SPOILAGE—DISCARD ANY JAR WITH THESE SYMPTOMS!

- The contents are leaking out the side.
- The top of the lid bulges and plinks when you push down on it.
- A bad odor.

- Mold growing inside.
- When you open a jar, the contents explode out.
- The contents look slimy and discolored.

Do not allow any animal or person to eat the contents. Reseal the jar and discard it safely in the garbage. Wash your hands thoroughly after handling the jars.

Relishes, pickles, chutneys and jars of tomatoes add a special sparkle to meals, make fine gifts and will be something to look forward to every year.

Equipment

- **Bowls:** Some acidic vegetables react with aluminum, altering the flavor and coloring the results. Bowls should be stainless steel, glass, ceramic or a heavy-weight plastic.

- **Colander:** Colanders come in a variety of sizes. They are convenient for washing, salting and draining vegetables.

- **Food Mill:** The best type quickly separates out the seeds and skin from the pulp. Food mills save a lot of time and effort.

- **Funnel:** A wide mouth canning funnel keeps the jar's rim clean while you are filling it.

- **Jars:** Canning jars use a heavier glass with a special two-part lid. They should not have any chips around the rim so the lid will seal properly. Jars come in sizes from half-pints to half-gallons with a narrow or wide-mouth neck.

- **Jar Lifter:** A set of specially designed tongs that make it easy to grab, hold and lift canning jars.

- **Labels:** Labels—homemade or decorative—should list the contents and the date made.

- **Ladles:** Look for the type with a spout on one side for easy pouring.

- **Timer:** Essential to accurately time the processing of vegetables.

- **Tongs:** Stainless steel tongs can pick up hot, sterilized lids.

- **Water-Bath Canner:** A kettle with a wire rack to hold jars. Make sure the kettle has the capacity to cover quart-size jars with an inch of water

- **Water-Steamer Canner :** A large kettle with a water reservoir that steams quart-size jars to process them safely.

Homemade pickles make a sweet gift, if you can bear to part with them.

Standard Directions for Boiling-Water Method of Preserving

Sterilizing the Jars and Lids

Always use new lids each time you seal a jar. The rubber on the lid is not dependable when reused. The screw bands can be reused as long as they are not bent or dented. The lids are sold separately.

Wash the jars before using them. Let them simmer on top of the stove for fifteen minutes. Use tongs to lift them out upside down so water drains out. The jars dry by themselves due to the extreme heat. Place them on a clean towel to prevent cracking.

Pour boiling water over the lids and bands, letting them sit for several minutes to soften the rubber seal. Use tongs to lift out the lids and bands, holding the lids only by the edges.

Sterilizing canning jars on the stove top.

Pouring boiling vinegar and salt over a mix of peppers, garlic, green beans and herbs.

Filling the Jars

Pack the vegetables in the jars as tightly as possible so that when you add the liquid it covers them and they cannot float up above the liquid. Pour the liquid over the vegetables according to the recipe's directions. The liquid is usually boiling hot, because you will water bath or steam the jars in the next step. Leave a half-inch space at the top of the jar.

Processing jars in a steam canner. Always follow specific recipe directions.

Sealing the Jars

Using a clean towel, wipe off the rim of the jar. Add the lid and the screw band and seal firmly, but not too tight.

Processing

Put the jars on a rack in a deep kettle half full of boiling water. Add more boiling water if necessary to cover the lids by 1 inch. Cover the pot, bring to a gentle boil and process according to the time indicated on the recipe. Add more boiling water if necessary to keep jars covered. When jars have finished process-

Using a canning basin. Use tongs and mitts, and be very careful of the hot steam!

Mixed Refrigerator Vegetable Pickles

This recipe lets you keep a jar of pickles in the refrigerator to pull out at a moment's notice. Add vegetables you want to pickle as you have room, putting in green tomatoes, okra, onions, cucumbers, beans, peppers, chiles, garlic or cauliflower. The vegetables need a couple of weeks to pickle. At the first of every month, make it a habit to renew the brine, pouring out the old and adding anew. Or, just start new jars when the old ones are filled.

1¼ cups water
1 cup 5-percent vinegar
1 tablespoon kosher or pickling salt
2 hot peppers, slit lengthwise
1 bay leaf
3 cloves garlic

2 large heads of dill
½ teaspoon mustard seeds
½ teaspoon cumin seeds
1 pound mixed vegetables, washed, seeded, pared and sliced into bite-sized pieces

In a non-reactive saucepan, boil together water, vinegar and salt. Stir until the salt has dissolved. Let the brining solution cool.

Add peppers, bay leaf, garlic, dill heads and seeds to a quart jar. Then pack the vegetables into the jar. Pour in the brining solution and seal the jar. Allow the mixture to season for at least 2 weeks in the refrigerator. Continue to refill the jar for 1 month. Then empty brine, mix up a new batch and refill the container.

ing, remove from canning kettle with canning tongs and place on a clean, folded towel.

Labeling and Storage

After 24 hours, check the seal of each jar by pressing on the center of the lid. If it stays down, the jar is correctly sealed. You can unscrew and remove the screw band. Label the jars with the ingredients and the date made. Store the jars in a cool, dark place.

Standard Directions for Steam Canner Method of Preservation

Fill the sterilized jars and seal as described above. Fill the bottom reservoir of the steam canner with water and bring to a boil. After the water boils place jars on the steamer rack.

Cover the pot, continue to boil and process according to the time indicated on the recipe. When opening the steam canner, lift off the top away from you to avoid injury from the steam. For best protection, wear oven mitts.

Author's Note: As research for this book, I purchased a steam canner. I find it much easier and quicker to use than the water bath canners, as the smaller amount of water in the steamer comes to boil quickly and is not so heavy and ponderous. However, I did burn my knuckles painfully the first time I used the steam canner by not following the directions and carelessly lifting the lid.

Homemade cornichons (baby cucumber pickles) with crusty French bread and pâté.

One reward: canned corn and peppers with that homegrown flavor.

Spicy Pickled Vegetables

Pick out vegetables which are all about the same size. Make sure they are super fresh and unblemished. You can make jars with just all beans or all squash, but it is more fun to pack jars with a mixture of different vegetables. Place the herbs and chiles around the outside of the jar for an elegant look.

3 to 4 pounds young vegetables such as okra, beans, baby squash or baby cucumbers
4 long, thin red chiles (fresh or dried)
6 large garlic cloves
1 tablespoon peppercorns
1 tablespoon coriander seeds

2 teaspoons mustard seeds
4 bay leaves
4 dill heads or 4 tablespoons dried dill seed
2½ cups water
2½ cups white wine vinegar
¼ cup salt

Trim and prepare vegetables so they fit into the jars, leaving ½ inch headroom. Sterilize jars and lids (see page 146). Let jars cool enough to handle. Divide the chiles, garlic and herbs among the four jars. Pack the jars with the vegetables.

In a medium-size saucepan, bring the water, vinegar and salt to a boil. Pour the hot brine over the vegetables, leaving ½ inch headroom. Wipe the edges of the jar clean and screw on the sterilized lid and band.

Process the jars in a boiling water bath or a steam canner for 12 minutes. Remove them from the canners and let them cool on a clean kitchen towel. After 24 hours, check lids for proper seal. Store any jars that did not seal in the refrigerator and use quickly. Store pickles in a cool dark place for 6 weeks to allow flavors to develop.

Makes 4 pints.

GRILLING AND ROASTING VEGETABLES

Grill eggplant slices just until they get "just brown" and have grid marks. They'll continue to cook after you take them off the grill.

For those who grew up on soggy, mushy vegetables, cooking without drowning them in buckets of boiling water will be a revelation in taste and texture.

Grilled or roasted vegetables have not had their flavors boiled out of them. Rather, a dry heat concentrates their flavors. If you are grilling, the slightly smoky touch of the fire adds a robust aroma to the rich, sweet, fresh vegetables.

Grilling Vegetables

Any vegetable sings with flavor when grilled. Carrots, tender little turnips, parsnips and even chard all can be grilled with success. If you wish, you can marinate your vegetables in a vinaigrette first, or just use a brush made from a sprig of rosemary to brush on olive oil. Make an herbal butter (see page 149) and toss the vegetables together with the butter when they come off the grill.

If you have never grilled corn, you are in for a treat. Strip back, but don't detach the husks. Remove the silk, brush a full-flavored olive oil or butter

---

Grilled peppers and lamb chunks with fresh rosemary.

Grilled Vegetable Ratatouille

This easy recipe uses quantities of grilled vegetables which are tossed together and served at room temperature with a light dressing of olive oil and just enough balsamic vinegar to bring out the flavors. Substitute other vegetables in the quantities you prefer.

1 round eggplant or 3 Japanese eggplants	6 tomatoes
4 red onions	4 ripe peppers
1 head of garlic	½ cup fruity olive oil
1 pound summer squash, zucchini, pattypan, crookneck or a mixture	Salt and pepper to taste
	Balsamic vinegar to taste

If you are using round eggplants, cut them into 1-inch thick slices. Peel and cut the onions in half. Remove the papery husk from the garlic head and cut off about 1 inch of the top.

Lightly oil the grill, grill the eggplants, summer squash, garlic, onions and tomatoes until they are cooked and tender. Move them around the grill so they don't scorch.

Grill the peppers until the skins are evenly charred. Place them in a paper bag and let them steam. When they have cooled, peel off the charred skin, remove the seeds and interior veins and cut them into 1-inch squares.

When they are cool enough to handle, slice all the vegetables into 1-inch chunks. Squeeze out the garlic meat and thin with olive oil to make a dressing. Use only as much garlic as you enjoy. Lightly toss the vegetables with the olive oil dressing. Add just enough balsamic vinegar to balance the flavors and then add salt and pepper to taste. Serve at room temperature.

Serves 4-6.

Winter Vegetable Roast

2 parsnips
2 sweet potatoes
4 carrots
10 small pink potatoes
6 turnips, about walnut size
4 small onions
6 cloves garlic
6 sage leaves
2 tablespoons olive oil
Salt and pepper to taste

Cut the parsnips in 1-inch rounds. Cut the larger pieces so they are all approximately the same size. Cut the sweet potatoes and carrots in similar-sized pieces.

Place all the vegetables and the sage in a large bowl. Pour in the olive oil and toss the vegetables with salt and pepper to thoroughly coat them. Place the vegetables in an oven roasting pan large enough to hold them in one layer.

Cover the pan with aluminum foil. Roast the vegetables in a 350°F oven until they are just beginning to become tender, about 30 minutes. Turn the vegetables with a spatula, then uncover and roast until the tops are brown and the vegetables are thoroughly tender, about 15 more minutes.

Serves 4-6.

Grilled napa cabbage is a different kind of barbecue pleaser.

over the surface and sprinkle with salt, pepper and thyme leaves. Pull the husk back over the corn cob and grill for 5 to 10 minutes, just until the corn is warmed through.

Roasting Vegetables

Roasting is another successful way to cook up garden-fresh vegetables. Baked in the oven, the dry heat intensifies the flavors, and when crisped or browned,

the sugars caramelize to add an additional richness.

The basic recipe is simplicity itself, and like any master recipe, easily accepts modifications. Adding bits of ham, prosciutto or bacon stretches the dish to a Sunday night supper. Dressing it up with cream and a cheese topping makes a fancier dish. Different herbs change the flavor from night to night.

All you have to do is oil an oven-proof pan and place the vegetables you have chosen to be roasted in a single layer. If the vegetables are very large or are of uneven sizes, cut them to equal shapes so they cook evenly. Toss them in the bowl with a bit of oil so they are

evenly coated. At the same time, salt and pepper them.

Splash a little water over the vegetables and shake the dish so the vegetables settle to one layer. Then cover the pan with foil.

Roast them in a 350°F oven until the vegetables are just beginning to become tender. Then uncover and continue to roast until the tops are brown and all the vegetables are fork tender.

If you want to add more flavor toss the cooked vegetables with herb butter (below) just before you serve them.

Grilling peppers brings out their sweetness. Avoid the seeds and membranes if you don't like spicy heat.

Herbed Butter

1 cup butter (2 sticks) at room temperature
2 teaspoons minced garlic
2 tablespoons minced Italian parsley
1 teaspoon fresh thyme
½ teaspoon fresh sage
1 teaspoon fresh rosemary
1 teaspoon freshly ground coarse pepper
3 tablespoons mixed dried edible flower petals such as calendula, rose petals and borage blossoms

In a food processor, thoroughly mix together the butter with the garlic, herbs and flower petals.

Turn out the butter mixture onto a piece of aluminum foil or plastic wrap. Using a wet spatula, shape the butter into a roll about 2 inches thick. Cover the roll with the foil or plastic wrap and then place the roll in a gallon-size plastic freezer bag. Freeze. To use, simply let the roll defrost just long enough to cut off the amount you need, and then refreeze.

STIR-FRIED VEGETABLES

A colorful, healthful summer stir-fry.

The Asian cooking technique of stir-frying uses high heat to quickly cook vegetables.

Make sure the pan is smoking hot before you add the oil. Give the seasonings a quick heating to release their flavors into the oil, then add the vegetables, stirring them around in the oil continuously. Add the cornstarch and water mixture last to the cooked vegetables, and cook just until the pan juices clear and thicken slightly.

Stir-frying works best with a round-bottomed wok widely

TIP   BE READY!

When doing a stir-fry, have all your vegetables prepared and sliced, for once you start the cooking, the dish is completed within minutes.

A Simple Summer Stir-Fry

Learning how to stir-fry opens new vistas for the cook who loves garden-fresh vegetables. Once you achieve the art of stir-frying, feel free to substitute ingredients. Just make sure to heat your gas ring or electric burner to its hottest temperature.

1 tablespoon peanut or canola oil
3 cloves garlic, peeled and finely chopped
1-inch knob of ginger, peeled and finely chopped
1 small piece dried orange peel
1 dried hot chile pepper, optional
1 carrot, sliced in dime-sized rounds
1 pound summer squash (about 3)—any mixture of zucchini, pattypan or crookneck, sliced in bite-sized pieces

½ pound snap beans (about 20), sliced diagonally in 1-inch pieces
2 ears of corn, kernels removed
2 tablespoons vegetable stock or water
1 tablespoon soy sauce
¼ teaspoon salt
1 teaspoon sugar
½ teaspoon cornstarch mixed with 1 teaspoon water
2 scallions, coarsely chopped

Heat the wok or sauté pan and add the oil. When the oil is hot, add the garlic, ginger, orange peel and the chile. Stir-fry for 30 seconds. Add the carrot and stir-fry for 1 minute, then add the squash, beans, and stock. Cover and continue to cook for 2 minutes. Uncover and add the soy sauce, salt and sugar. Cook for 1 minute. Add the corn and the cornstarch and stir until the sauce thickens. Turn the stir-fry out on a warmed platter and garnish with the scallions sprinkled over the top.

Serves 4 as a side dish.

Fresh garden vegetables, chopped and ready for stir-frying.

available in hardware and kitchen stores, but in a pinch a large sauté pan can substitute.

Once you have mastered the basic stir-fry technique, you can stir up any combination of vegetables. Just remember to cook the firmest vegetables first, as they will need to cook longer than softer vegetables.

Don't overcook the vegetables. They should remain crisp, not raw. Stir-fried greens are particularly delicious, including iceberg or romaine lettuce.

Stir-fry 101: the versatile wok and spatula.

Ken Hom's Mock Vegetable Pasta

The Chinese-American chef Ken Hom created an ingenious use for zucchini in this recipe. If you have a mandoline or vegetable slicer, the zucchini slices up much faster. This is a good use for zucchini which missed harvesting at a smaller size. If you choose, you can always use spaghetti squash in place of the zucchini. Finish the dish as he does—with garlic, ginger, soy sauce and chopped coriander; or as in this recipe, toss the stir-fried "pasta" with pesto.

2 pounds zucchini (about 6 medium size); the longer the zucchini, the longer the pasta
1 tablespoon salt
1 teaspoon olive oil
2 tablespoons finely chopped garlic
4 tablespoons pesto (see page 143)
Salt and pepper to taste
¼ teaspoon chile seeds or chile powder
2 tablespoons freshly grated Parmesan cheese

With a knife, a mandoline or vegetable slicer, cut the zucchini in long strips as thin as spaghetti. Place the zucchini in a colander and toss with the salt. Let it drain in the colander for 20 minutes, then rinse briefly and squeeze out any liquid in a clean dish towel.

Heat a wok or sauté pan and add the oil. When the oil is hot, add the garlic and stir-fry for 30 seconds. Turn in the zucchini and stir-fry for 4 minutes, or until the zucchini is cooked. Turn off the heat, add the pesto and toss. Add a bit of olive oil if the mixture seems too dry. Salt and pepper to taste. Turn out on a platter and dust with the chile seeds or powder and the Parmesan.

Serves 4 as a side dish.

BAKING WITH VEGETABLES

Zucchini Pancakes

Make these pancakes as a brunch dish or to accompany grilled meats. Topped with crème fraîche and grilled zucchini for a double flavor hit. These 'cakes are delicious, with a delicate texture that is mouthwateringly memorable.

3 medium zucchini, about 4 to 6
  inches long
1 teaspoon salt
2 eggs
2 tablespoons fruity olive oil
1 cup all-purpose flour
1 teaspoon baking powder
½ teaspoon salt
1 teaspoon fresh thyme
¼ cup milk

Grate the zucchini, toss with the salt and place in a colander for 10 to 15 minutes to draw off the water. Then rinse the zucchini briefly in fresh water, drain, and press dry with a clean kitchen towel.

In a medium-sized bowl, combine the eggs and the olive oil. Beat well for 1 to 2 minutes. Add the zucchini and stir well to combine.

In a small bowl, combine the flour, baking powder, salt and thyme. Stir well. Add the flour, in small amounts, to the zucchini mixture alternately with the milk. Do not over mix. If there are small lumps of flour, it does not matter.

Spoon the pancake batter onto a hot griddle or into a large skillet. Cook over medium heat until set. Flip the pancakes to finish cooking on the other side.

Serve the pancakes topped with crème fraîche and sautéed zucchini.

Serves 4 as a side dish.

Magical results happen when vegetables are used in baking cakes, muffins, breads and fritters. The vegetables add texture, moisture and flavor that transforms what could be mundane into something splendid. Experiment with these classic recipes. You might even deny your-self fresh sautéed vegetables to make some of these scrumptious baked goods.

Baking with squash makes for delicious results.

Homemade herb butter on fresh baked bread.

Polenta Carrot Cake

This is an update of classic carrot cake, using cornmeal, a whole orange and olive oil. Instead of the typical dark carrot cake, this one is golden yellow with flecks of orange—from the whole ground-up orange and the carrots themselves. A really delicious dessert cake!

2 cups unbleached all-purpose flour
1 cup polenta or cornmeal
1 teaspoon salt
1 teaspoon baking soda
1/2 teaspoon baking powder
1 1/2 teaspoons cinnamon
1 cup olive oil

1 medium-size orange, quartered
2 cups sugar
3 eggs, at room temperature
2 cups grated raw carrots
Confectioner's sugar for dusting

Preheat the oven to 350°F.

In a large mixing bowl, combine the flour, polenta, salt, baking soda, baking powder and cinnamon. Mix well.

In the bowl of a food processor or in a blender, add the oil and the orange quarters. Blend until the orange has been ground to small shreds. Add the eggs and sugar and process for 2 minutes. Then add the carrots and continue to blend until the carrots are in small shreds.

Combine the carrot mixture with the dry mixture, stirring just until it all is moistened.

Thoroughly oil a bundt pan. Add the cake mixture to the pan and place it on the middle rack of the oven. Bake the cake for 1 hour or until the edges pull away from the sides of the pan and a toothpick inserted in the center comes out clean.

Cool the cake on a rack for 10 minutes, then unmold and thoroughly cool. Dust the top with confectioner's sugar.

Yellow Squash Muffins

2 pounds yellow crookneck squash (about 3 medium squash), to make 2 cups grated squash
2 eggs, well beaten
1 cup oil
1 cup sugar
3 cups all-purpose flour
1 1/2 tablespoons baking powder
1 teaspoon cinnamon
1/2 teaspoon dried thyme
1 teaspoon salt

Preheat the oven to 350°F.

Grate the squash and measure out 2 cups.

In a medium bowl, beat together the squash, eggs, oil and sugar. In a separate bowl, combine the flour, baking powder, cinnamon, thyme and salt. Add the dry ingredients to the squash mixture, stirring just until they are moistened. Do not over mix.

Pour the ingredients into a greased muffin tin. Bake on the middle rack of the oven for 35 minutes or until the muffins are golden brown.

Makes 12 muffins.

SOURCES

Cook's Garden
P.O. Box 535
Londonderry, VT 05148
802-824-3400
Excellent lettuce varieties and
    mesclun blends.

Filaree Farms
Rt. Box 162
Okanogan, WA 08840-9774
509-422-6940
Specializing in garlic varieties.

Johnny's Selected Seeds
Foss Kill Road
Albion, ME 04910
207-437-4301
Excellent variety of seeds, often
    at the lowest prices.

Kitazawa Seed Company
1111 Chapman Street
San Jose, CA 95126
408-243-1330
Unusual Asian vegetable seeds.

Nichols Garden Nursery
1190 North Pacific Highway
Albany, OR 97321
541-928-9280

Pinetree Garden Seeds
Box 300
New Gloucester, ME 04260
207-926-3400
A good mix of hybrid and open-
    pollinated seeds, tested for
    the home gardener.

**Irish Eyes with a Hint of
Garlic**
P.O. Box 307
Ellensburg, WA 98926
509-925-6025
Unusual potatoes and garlic
    varieties.

Seeds Blüm
Idaho City Stage
Boise, ID 83706
FAX 208-338-5658
Many different varieties of
    open-pollinated plants and
    heirloom varieties

Shepherd's Garden Seeds
30 Irene Street
Torrington, CT 06790
203-482-3638

Unusual varieties carefully
    chosen for taste and finest
    flavor.

**Southern Exposure Seed
Exchange**
P.O. Box 170
Earlysville, VA 22936
804-973-8717
Organically grown seeds of
    heirloom varieties.

Territorial Seed Company
20 Palmer Avenue
Cottage Grove, OR 97424
541-942-9547
Short-season varieties that
    thrive in cooler summer
    climates or for spring and fall
    planting.

**Tomato Growers Supply
Company**
P.O. Box 720
Fort Myers, FL 33902
941-768-1119
Many unusual tomato varieties
    for all climates.

SOURCES FOR INFORMATION ABOUT HERBS

Herb Society of America
9019 Kirtland Chardon,
    Mentor, OH 44060,
    216-256-0514.

The Herb Companion. Interweave Press, Inc.
201 East Fourth Street, Loveland, Colorado 80537
    303-669-7672.
Subscriptions to this bimonthly magazine are $21. A
    very informative magazine filled with articles about
    growing and using herbs.

BOOKS ON VEGETABLE GARDENING

Coleman, Eliot. *The New Organic Grower's Four Season Harvest.* Chelsea Green Press, 1992.

Creasy, Rosalind. *Cooking from the Garden.* San Francisco, CA: Sierra Club Books, 1988.

Kourik, Robert. *Designing and Maintaining Your Edible Landscape Naturally.* Metamorphic Press, 1986.

Kourik, Robert. *Drip Irrigation for Every Landscape and All Climates.* Metamorphic Press, 1992.

INDEX OF PLANTS

GENERAL INDEX

Photo Credits

Michael Landis

Additional photography courtesy of :
   Mowers Photography: pp. 5 all, 14 LR, 15 (2: UR, LR), 54 UR, 59 UR, 68 LR, 69 UR, 72 LL, 76 UR, 78 UR, 81 UR, 90 LR, 92 (2: UR, LR), 100 UR, 101 LR, 103 LR, 104 T, 111 (2: UR, B), 112 LR, 114 UR, 115 UR, 130 UR, 137 UR, 144 T, 152 LR; **David Brus/The Garden Archive:** pp. 12 LR, 21 UR, 22 UR, 27 UL, 88 UR; **Walter Chandoha:** pp. 13 LL, 33 (2: LR, LL), 34 UL, 36 UR, 37 LR, 38 all, 39 R, 40 UR, 46-47, 53 T, 92 UL, 98 R, 119 T, 121 UR, 126 LR, 127 B; **David Cavagnaro:** pp. 39 L, 40 (2: L, LR), 41 (2: LL, LR), 74 UL, 76 LL, 77 T, 88 LR, 89 LR, 94 LR, 106 UL, 110, 125 UL; **Jeff Johnson/The Garden Archive:** pp. 55 UL, 56 UL, 61 LR, 63 L, 71 UL, 78 B, 80 LR, 85 LR, 87 LL, 106 UR, 109 B, 118 B, 130 LL, 145, 148 LL.

Illustrations

   Bill Reynolds/K&K Studios: pp. 13, 17, 19 both, 21, 22 both, 25 both, 30 all, 31; **Nancy Wirsig McClure/Hand-to-Mouse Arts:** pp. 12, 20.

A Special Thank You To:

Joshua Landis
Latisha Landis
Patricia Kremer
Staglin Family Vineyard
Araujo Estate Wines
Ironhorse Vineyards
Kendall Jackson Winery
Forni Brown
Floyd Lumas
Jeff Dawson
Harmony Farms
Cakebread Cellars